The Healing Marriage

Principles and prayers
for flourishing couples

Daniel and Esther Baumgartner

Bethesda Heilungsdienst

Title:	The Healing Marriage: Principles and prayers for flourishing couples

Original title: Die heilsame Ehe: Einsichten und Gebete für glückliche Paare
Translation by Esther Baumgartner

Print: ISBN 978-3-9525900-0-3
Ebook: ISBN 978-3-9525900-1-0

Published by: Verein Bethesda Heilungsdienst, Zurich
info@bethesda-heilungsdienst.ch
www.bethesda-heilungsdienst.ch

Editorial & design: Bethesda Heilungsdienst & David M. Taylor, soundswrite.ch
Illustrations: Claudia Huber, claudiahuber-illustration.de
Proofreading: Elisabeth Taylor

This book is based on the "Die heilsame Ehe", radio course broadcast on Radio Maria Switzerland in 2021.

Disclaimer: The names mentioned in the testimonials and examples have been changed to protect the confidentiality of the individuals. The generic examples were created for this book and are based on our extensive prayer ministry experience. Readers are responsible for adapting the material to their individual situation and marriage. This is a self-help book with advice on marriage and relationships and prayers for self use. It assumes a spiritual worldview that is consistent with the teachings of the New Testament. Prayer for deliverance has been practiced by followers of Christ throughout history. It has always been a controversial topic. Readers must exercise discernment in the way they apply the contents of this book. The authors and Verein Bethesda Heilungsdienst disclaim all responsibility for any loss, damage, or disruption due to errors or omissions in the information and advice given in this book, whether such errors or omissions result from negligence, accident, or any other cause. The authors insist on the importance of accurately discerning the difference between spiritual, emotional, and physical issues and explicitly advise readers to take into account the advice of relevant specialists, including physicians, psychologists, or counselors.

Endorsements

"I buy 'Parents Empowered', Daniel and Esther's book on healing and deliverance with kids and teens, in bulk because I believe it is the one book that every parent needs to read. It is the book I wish I had when I was raising my children. So it's no surprise that their new book, 'The Healing Marriage', is the one book I wish I had when I was a young bride. I love how the book can be used as a devotion, as a pre-marital counselling resource, or as a guide navigating couples through the tough spots. I expect this book to be a staple in my ministry and will recommend it as a wedding gift for newlyweds."
– *Lisa Piper, Founder of Miracle of Deliverance & Assistant Pastor at The River Church, Kentucky, USA*

"I am so grateful to Daniel and Esther for 'The Healing Marriage'. It is a unique resource offering concrete help to consolidate and strengthen marriages. In a time when marriage is so often discussed in terms of crisis, or the concept of marriage as a whole is subject to reinterpretation, this is a book well worth reading – and more importantly, applying.

Every couple has its share of problems and goes through difficulties from time to time, but Daniel and Esther believe that there are always ways to grow together and avoid drifting apart. Drawing on years of experience, they equip couples to find those ways and move forward and thrive together. Their deep faith and knowledge of God's Word help us to better understand the heart of God for marriage and what is available to us in Christ.

'The Healing Marriage' is also an invitation to self-reflection on key areas of married life, and inspires hope through practical examples of relationships that have been renewed

and restored. It helps readers to see where they have failed or made mistakes, whilst at the same time opening up paths for forgiveness and healing. Thus reading 'The Healing Marriage' can be likened to a visit to a spa or a health resort; it helps remove impurities, refreshes and enables couples to experience greater beauty and deeper satisfaction in their relationship."
– Father Thomas Rellstab, Former Director of Radio Maria Switzerland

"The sort of intimacy that a marriage gives will expose the wounds of the past and any moral weaknesses of the couple. We all need forgiveness, guidance, and support, and the best guides and practical advice that we can receive is from those who have travelled this exciting but perilous journey before us. Daniel and Esther Baumgartner are experienced guides and they have written 'The Healing Marriage' not only to share their own challenges and successes but also to help other couples achieve healthy life-affirming and life-giving relationships.

Following the practical help offered in this guide, and using the prayers, couples can discover forgiveness for the past, healing for the present and deliverance for their future together. Marriage is not only good for couples, it is also fundamental and essential to a flourishing society. A healthy society needs healthy marriages, and this guide can help."
– Rev Dr Samuel Randall, Director Radio Maria Australia, & Mrs Mirjam Randall

Testimonials

"*The Healing Marriage* has been a real eye-opener for us as a couple. Our relationship with God, the third person in our marriage, has deepened as a result. The authors show in a lively and humorous way how spiritual and emotional wounds can be at the heart of misunderstandings and dissatisfaction in marriage. The deeply Christian insights and prayers they offer for dealing with these issues are practical and effective. This book is a gift for couples of all ages". – D & U

"This wonderful book was hard to put down. It has helped us to identify the roots of many personal issues that have negatively affected our marriage from the start. Using the practical prayer tools in the book has brought tremendous change in these key areas of our relationship. We have been touched by the wisdom and grace of the Lord flowing to us from the pages of this divinely inspired book. Rather than feeling condemned by past mistakes or overwhelmed by what still needs to change, the invitation to pause for prayer and reflection at the end of each chapter has enabled us to break through and find peace and a deep sense of inner wellbeing". – E & H

"The bite-sized chapters contain many powerful insights and are perfect for slower readers. We have both benefited from the many valuable and practical ideas in the book. We have found the concepts and prayer steps easy to understand and to apply". – A & S

Acknowledgments

Father Thomas, former programme director of Radio Maria Switzerland. We had been planning to write a book on marriage when you called with an urgent request for a radio course to help couples struggling with the effects of the ongoing covid pandemic. We knew it was the Holy Spirit urging us to give voice to the message that had been forming in our hearts. We ended up writing the programmes as we went along, which was nerve-wracking at times, but a thrilling ride nonetheless. The Lord blessed the radio course and we decided to base the book on it! Thank you for making the pioneer broadcasts possible, and for the support of your team.

Elisabeth Taylor. Your editing and proofreading skills have sharpened the message. Your encouragement, wisdom and motherly love have helped us through difficult project phases.

David M. Taylor. Your editorial, design and spiritual support has once again made all the difference.

Our friends and partners at Bethesda Heilungsdienst. Some of you were at our wedding, others connected later. But the love, prayers and support of all of you keep us strong.

Above all our loving Heavenly Father. Thank you for your amazing gift of our marriage, a healing marriage made in heaven! You brought us together and have helped us build a relationship beyond anything we could have hoped for, or achieved on our own.

Preface

After graduating in theology, Daniel was part of a mission team to Argentina. He was a speaker at a healing seminar in Buenos Aires. A doctor and counsellor who attended the meetings heard that he was engaged to be married. He took Daniel aside, looked him straight in the eye and said:

"Daniel, marriage is a wonderful and holy institution designed by God to bring us great joy and happiness! Don't ever let anyone tell you otherwise!"

Daniel has never forgotten these words. They deeply impacted and encouraged him. We have been happily married for almost 30 years now. And we have found that marriage not only brings us great joy and deep satisfaction, but can also be a place of tremendous healing!

We want to share with you some of the valuable insights we have gained over the years from our own marriage that have made this possible. And, as prayer counsellors, our experience of listening to others and seeing their lives transformed by the same prayers and insights we share here has motivated us to write this book and share them with you.

Whether you are preparing for marriage, recently married or have been married for many years, we pray that as you read this book, do the exercises and pray the prayers, your vision for marriage, your love and commitment to each other will grow and your relationship will flourish.

Introduction

The concept behind this book is very simple. We believe that couples can learn to pray for each other for forgiveness, healing and deliverance. And in doing so, things that may not be going so well in a relationship can actually get better. The idea that we can pray for and with each other may be new to you, especially if you are not used to praying as a couple on a deeper level, or maybe even at all. But don't worry! As you progress through the book, you will learn and practice using simple, specific and effective principles and prayers that open doors to greater wholeness, contentment and joy together.

Our approach is based on five healing and freedom prayer tools that couples can use to pray for each other. Learning to pray for each other in this way was a new discovery for us back in the early days of our marriage. But as we saw the transformative power of these prayers in our own relationship, we began to offer them to couples who came to us for counselling. We found that they worked for many of them too!

We want to share these life-changing insights and prayer tools with you. If you are looking to enrich your marriage and grow in love and unity, or are struggling to overcome certain issues threatening to drive you apart, we believe this approach will help you. As you work through the chapters with an open heart and mind, God can touch you and meet your needs.

Consider the following Bible verse:

> *Therefore, if anyone is in Christ, the new creation has come: The old has gone, the new is here!* (2 Cor. 5:17)

When we come to Christ as husband and wife, we can stand on this promise that we are a new creation in Christ. He creates new things in us, and that includes new things in our marriage. This has been our experience. Everything can be made new when we come to him. Not necessarily overnight; it is often a process. But the important thing is that we come to him first.

We are amazed when we look back at how God has helped us to overcome many difficulties in our own marriage. As we applied ourselves to studying the Word of God and trained ourselves to come to him, listening for the voice of his Holy Spirit, he helped us to identify the spiritual and emotional roots of the problems that were spoiling our relationship and hindering our unity. We then used the healing and freedom prayers to pray for each other and experienced lasting results. We became increasingly excited about what can be achieved when we make space for the Holy Spirit to speak to us and then pray about what he shows us. There really is tremendous power in prayer!

The prayer tools we present in this book are simple and powerful. You can adapt and use them again and again as the Holy Spirit leads you to the root of your problems in the key areas of sins, hurts and demonic oppression. As well as being a guide to effective prayer, this book is also a workbook. We've included questions and additional template prayers designed to help you reflect on the material and apply the principles to your situation. Doing so will enable you to take steps and make progress.

Lastly, if you want your marriage to flourish, you may also need to learn new skills, like how to communicate and listen better. Being willing to admit where you are wrong, rather than finding fault with others. Putting things right when you make a mess of things. Learning to become one at a deeper level. And how to recognise hurts and areas of spiritual bondage and pray effectively for healing and deliverance.

Contents

UNITY   1

1. **One heart and soul**   3
    In search of a deeper connection

2. **The power of the marriage covenant**   7
    God is for us

3. **A new creation**   11
    Two become one

4. **Identifying obstacles to unity**   17
    Institutionalized chaos

5. **Overcoming obstacles to unity**   23
    Introduction to the prayer tools

6. **Six tips for growing in unity**   29
    Inspiration for daily life

COMMUNICATION   33

7. **Laying the right foundations**   35
    Communication enables relationship

8. **Prioritising Communication**   39
    Good communication is contested

9. **Overcoming our differences**   43
    When two worlds collide

10. **Communication killers**   47
What to watch out for

11. **From battlefields to radio silence**   53
Exposing communication abuse

12. **Communication and conflict resolution**   57
Inspiration moving forward

RESTORATION   63

13. **Nowhere to hide**   65
Facing what's inside

14. **Recognising sin in marriage**   71
Destructive behavior patterns

15. **Overcoming sin in marriage**   79
Five steps that bring life

16. **Prayer tool for restoration**   85
The Forgiveness Prayers for couples

17. **Hitting the target**   89
Learning to resist and stay connected

HEALING   93

18. **The power of healing in marriage**   95
Called to heal one another

19. **Breaking negative patterns of hurt**   101
Change is possible

20. Healing past and present wounds   107
The Hurts Prayers for couples

21. Dealing with negative reactions   113
The Reactions Prayers for couples

22. When memories torment us The   117
Memories Prayers for couples

DELIVERANCE   121

23. The power of deliverance in marriage   123
A key to tangible change

24. The spiritual realm around us   127
God gives us the victory

25. Identifying and closing entry points   133
Preparing for freedom

26. Praying for deliverance in marriage   139
The Deliverance Prayers for couples

27. Getting better results   143
Combining prayer tools

APPENDIX   147

Unity

Learning to become one

One heart and soul
In search of a deeper connection

Lasting love is something that most people naturally dream of. No matter how many disappointments we may have experienced or observed, we still yearn for someone who will understand and love us, and whom we can love in return – a partner and friend with whom we can build a stable life and who will stand by us in good times and in bad. But beneath this desire lies a deeper need for a heart connection. We long to know and be known on a deeper level.

For many couples, however, there is a disconnect between what we hoped and dreamed for when we got married and what we actually experience in daily life. While we may feel connected and enjoy wonderful unity in some areas of life, others are overshadowed by the underlying tension of disunity or outright disagreements. Can you relate to this?

Maybe you've worked as hard as you can on your marriage, but certain tensions remain. "Well, I guess that's married life," you conclude. "After all, every family has their problems!" You may have even given up on the original dream.

Having counseled many couples and being still happily married after twenty-seven years, we can assure you that you are not alone and the good news is, there is hope! With the right help, insights and tools, it really is possible to overcome the division, grow that connection and find unity and peace in every area of married life!

We have found that marital satisfaction has much to do with the ability to grow into deeper unity together. The more united and connected we are on all levels, the more satisfied we will be with our marriage. So how can we remove any obstacles to unity and grow together as a couple? This is perhaps the most important question we can ask ourselves, and it is at the heart of *The Healing Marriage*.

God's heart for couples

Some people are scared by the idea of unity or oneness in marriage. It makes them feel trapped or suffocated. There are many reasons why someone might feel this way. Often such feelings are linked to negative experiences in the past. We will look at this later and discover how God can help us to overcome such experiences. The important thing to understand here is that God's heart and original design for marriage is for husbands and wives to complement, strengthen and enjoy each other.

You may have noticed the picture at the beginning of this section of a couple in a small boat together. Tandem kayaking is a great illustration of unity in marriage. It requires disciplined co-operation as well as practice and perseverance. Both paddlers need to take on certain tasks and responsibilities. But by working together, they can control both the direction and speed of their kayak. And a well-coordinated team can cover amazing distances together – and have a great time!

So how can we learn to 'paddle' in such a way that we move forward together, even when daily life is rough and demanding? How can we stay united and avoid going round in circles, or worse, ending up in different boats altogether?

There can be many reasons for discord and disunity. In this book, based on our own experience and our work with couples over many years, we will identify four key areas and address them one by one. Besides the familiar topic of marital communication, couples need to understand what sin is and why it can damage a relationship. Then there are emotional hurts that make change very difficult, and finally we will address the spiritual dimension. Talking about the unseen world in the context of marriage might be new to you. But we believe it is important and nothing to be afraid of.

The sections of the book are therefore: unity, communication, restoration, healing, and deliverance. As we move through each topic, we will equip you with practical strategies and simple, proven prayer tools to use in each area. As you learn to use them, we believe your unity as a couple will grow and you will experience greater peace and happiness together.

Pause for thought

- What does unity in marriage mean to you?
- In what areas are you already connected and united?
- What difference might greater unity make to your marriage?

Chapter 2

The power of the marriage covenant
God is for us

Marriage is sometimes discussed as a model for regulating the legal status and property of two people who wish to join their lives together. But it is so much more! Did you know that marriage is actually a sacred covenant – a binding promise or agreement defining obligations and commitments – that God himself enters into with us? It is his presence and commitment in marriage that make the difference:

> *A cord of three strands is not quickly broken.*
> (Ecclesiastes 4:12b)

This verse is engraved on our wedding rings to remind us that our union is not just based on our decision to be together. Or even on our legal status as a couple, but on a powerful covenant entered into with each other and the Lord. *He* is the third strand in the cord of our marriage. The beauty of being in a covenant relationship with God is that he is unchanging. He promises to be faithful – even when we are unfaithful:

> *If we are faithless, he remains faithful, for he cannot disown himself.* (2 Timothy 2:13)

The amazing thing about this covenant is that it can be renewed at any time, no matter where we are as a couple or how much we may have failed. This is good news, not only for those of us already married, but for anyone considering marriage! Because God is the third party in our marriage, we can always build new and better foundations together. He will help us! And just as he loves us, is faithful to us and fights for us, so we too can be loving, faithful and fight for one another.

Some people float into marriage on a rosy cloud of romantic feelings and enthusiasm, but have little experience of building unity and solid relationships. When tensions and difficulties arise, they feel frustrated, disappointed and overwhelmed. Their love for their partner diminishes and their faith in their marriage is shaken. Their focus begins to shift from their partner back to themselves. If resignation or despair sets in and spreads, the relationship is likely to grow cold or even break down altogether. But if we understand the nature of the marriage covenant, and that God is for us and present with us things can begin to change.

Imitating the example of Christ

If we are honest, most of us probably had a sprinkling of self-interest mixed in to our decision to get married. We may still tend to think much more about ourselves, than about our partner! It is not always easy to choose to focus on the needs of others, especially when many around us are becoming increasingly self-absorbed. But there really is no place for selfishness in the marriage covenant. Self-centredness drains us, weakens our unity and can cause tremendous damage.

God's heart and his motivation for entering into covenant with us, however, are totally different, as the example of our Lord Jesus Christ clearly shows.

Talking about himself, Jesus said:

"For even the Son of Man did not come to be served, but to serve and to give His life as a ransom for many." (Mark 10:45)

In Philippians chapter 2 verses 5-11, the apostle Paul describes how Jesus, though he was God and King of the universe, humbled himself and took the form of a lowly servant. Most monarchs would never dream of changing places with one of their servants – but that is exactly what Jesus did! He left his throne and came into this world, not to rule, but to serve. He offers us an alternative to our selfishness and self-centredness. He models the heart and attitude of a true servant and shows us a better way to live.

If we want to (re)capture our partner's heart, and grow in love and connection together, we would do well to imitate Christ's example. Instead of clinging to our rights and waiting like kings and queens to be served at home, we need to step down from our thrones and ask: "What is best for my spouse?" As we let go of our selfishness and learn to serve one another in humility, as Christ did, and in the strength he provides, our love and unity will grow.

Pause for thought

- What difference does it make to you to know that your marriage is based on a sacred covenant?

- Where have you been selfish in your marriage?

- How can you love and serve your partner, following the example of Jesus?

Where necessary, ask your partner's forgiveness.
You can say: *"My dearest ....(name). I am sorry that I have often put myself first and been selfish. Please forgive me!"*

Chapter 3

A new creation
Two become one

God creates something new through the marriage covenant. This covenant is between God, a husband and wife. No one else is. For many of us, however, marriage feels a bit more crowded than that! It's as if there are all sorts of other people in the marriage that we don't feel quite free from. They could be parents or parents-in-law, siblings, close friends or even former partners etc. It is important to take an honest look at our marriage and to pray for freedom if we don't feel free.

In this chapter we focus on two key areas: Our relationship with our parents and freedom from previous sexual partners. However, you can apply the same principles and prayers to many other relationships as well.

Relationships with parents

As we noted earlier, in the eyes of God, a marriage is always a new creation. In Genesis 2:24 we read:

> *That is why a man leaves his father and mother and*
> *is united to his wife, and they become one flesh.*

God's design in marriage, therefore, is that a man and woman, having left their mother and father, form a deep and intimate union with each other. We have found that many problems in marriage have their roots in the fact that either the husband or the wife, or both, are not completely free from their parents on an emotional or spiritual level. Tensions can arise between spouses as a result of this lack of freedom.

Often the problem is not even that the parents or parents-in-law don't want to let their married children go. Rather, for whatever reason, the daughter or son does not feel completely free from the parents. As a result, he or she cannot grow into deeper unity with their spouse, as God intended. But leaving our parents and being joined to our spouse is crucial to achieving unity together.

Most parents mean well and want the best for us, even after we leave home. Their advice is often well-intentioned. But a couple must learn to make their own decisions without feeling pressured or manipulated by parents or in-laws.

Questions:

- Do you feel emotionally free in relation to your parents?
- Is your partner free in relation to his or her parents?

If either of you doesn't feel free in your relationship with your parents, you may need to pray and cut any unhelpful spiritual or emotional ties with them. When we pray in this way, we are not saying that our parents have done everything wrong. Nor are we passing judgment on them. We are not rejecting them as people, abandoning them, or cutting them out of our lives. The point is simply that we can only be fully joined and united as a couple if we first leave our parents. This leaving includes feeling free to organise our own lives and make our own decisions, even in the face of well-meaning advice or perceived interference.

Once we are emotionally and spiritually free from our parents and parents-in-law, we can set healthy boundaries together. We will also be able to respond with appropriate love and respect when we see a boundary being crossed. The same principle applies to other relationships. The ability to set boundaries together on different levels is very important if we are to enjoy and maintain a deeper unity.

Prayer:

Praying together for freedom can be very helpful and make a big difference. We have found that even couples who have been married for years may not feel completely free from their parents. But the following prayer can bring peace and unity, and it's never too late to pray it. You can say:

> *"In the name of Jesus Christ, I cut all soul ties and connections between myself and my parents in the spiritual realm that are not of God. I declare that I am now married and living in union with my husband/wife as part of a new creation made by God and in covenant with him. We are now a separate and distinct family. I thank you, Lord, for my parents and bless them in Jesus' name."*

Freedom from previous sexual partners

Good sex in marriage revives and refreshes the relationship, bringing a sense of overall wellbeing, satisfaction, security and belonging. This, in turn, increases our unity and infuses both partners with new strength and life. Because sex is so powerful, the apostle Paul urges married couples not to neglect it and not to get into the habit of not sleeping together:

Do not deprive each other except perhaps by mutual consent and for a time, so that you may devote yourselves to prayer. Then come together again so that Satan will not tempt you because of your lack of self-control. (1 Corinthians 7:5)

Paul isn't talking about having sex on command. We're human beings, not robots, so it's important to take time to create a romantic atmosphere where we both feel comfortable, can open up and experience desire for each other. Sex is also influenced by what is going on in our relationship in general. Good communication, dealing swiftly with hurts between us and forgiving each other quickly all help to promote an atmosphere where satisfying sex can happen and we deal with these areas in later sections.

The focus of this chapter is on becoming one, but this can still be difficult to achieve if we are not free from previous sexual partners. This is because when we have sex outside the protective framework of the marriage covenant, ungodly soulties are created. Spirits that are not of God can also come into our lives through the other person. This disturbs our sense of inner freedom. Our partner may also feel that someone or something is interfering with our connection.

Therefore, if we have had previous sexual partners, it is important to cut any emotional and spiritual ties between ourselves so that we can be fully united to our husband or wife as God intended.

Question:

- Do you feel free from any previous sexual partners?

Prayer:

If you do not feel free, we invite you to pray the following prayer:

> *"Jesus, I'm sorry I had sex with .... Please forgive*
> *me and cleanse me. In your name, I cut myself loose*
> *from (name, if known)...... in the spiritual world*
> *and break any ungodly soul-tie with them. I tell*
> *every spirit that has entered me through this relation-*
> *ship to leave me now in the name of Jesus."*

Often people feel a pressure in their body when they pray this prayer, followed by a lightness or sense of freedom when they think of the former partner. Repeat this prayer for each person or situation the Holy Spirit brings to your mind until you feel completely free. If you still have hurts from previous relationships, these also need to be healed. We look at how to do this in the section on healing.

Chapter 4

Identifying obstacles to unity
Institutionalized chaos

Just as tandem kayakers can easily lose their paddling rhythm if distracted, so couples can suddenly find themselves out of sync for many reasons. Identifying what has disrupted our unity is the first step in restoring it. In this chapter we look at how language and cultural differences, lies and negative behaviour patters can constantly sabotage our efforts to be more united. Once we understand what's going on, things can begin to change.

Language and cultural differences

We have four different cultures and three nationalities in our marriage mix! Daniel is from Switzerland, Esther is British-Swiss and was born and spent her formative years in Kenya. We moved to Argentina soon after we got married. We ended up staying for ten years and our three children were born there. This variety of cultures and languages has certainly spiced things up and made our lives more interesting, but it has also meant that we have had to work extra hard to achieve the level of unity we enjoy as a couple and family today. Learning to understand each other was not always easy, especially in the early years of our marriage – and to be honest, we still struggle at times!

Language is a funny thing. Have you ever noticed how you can say one thing and the person you're talking to understands something completely different, often without either of you realising it? Daniel's parents like to tell the story of the first time his mother met his father's family. Now his mother is from Zurich and his father from Bern. If you know anything about Switzerland, you will know that these are actually two culturally and linguistically different regions, even though they share the same basic language and are just over an hour apart! After church on Sunday, someone approached Daniel's mother and said in thick Bernese, "I've heard a lot about you. Nothing but good things!" But his mother understood, "I've heard a lot about you. Not all good things!" She was shocked and thought, "Oh, no, what on earth have I done to make people think so badly of me...?" Imagine her relief when she found out that it was all a linguistic misunderstanding. And that everyone loved her!

Linguistic and cultural differences have the potential to keep us from growing into deeper unity, so it is worth taking the time to reflect on any differences and to work at really trying to understand each other. If you are struggling with cultural or linguistic challenges in your marriage, be encouraged! Unity is possible – even in cross-cultural or multilingual marriages. It may just take a little more faith, patience and determination to make it work!

When lying is a problem

One day we were sitting in a cafe, enjoying a quiet moment, when an elderly couple came in and sat down at the table next to ours. After a while, the woman suddenly said in a loud voice, "You know, you've been lying to me about so many things lately. I don't believe a word you say anymore!" We have met many people who, like this man, take the truth with a pinch of salt. Lying is no big deal to them. But we believe that this attitude to telling the truth is one of the reasons why so many relationships fail. Because if you don't really know what happened in a given situation that caused hurt, loss or chaos, then it's hard to agree on who should apologise to whom and for what. And it is even harder to forgive each other and move forward together in peace, unity and trust.

Lies tend to leave a trail of frustration, bitterness and hurt. These negative reactions, in turn, can fester within us, laying the groundwork for further discord. Telling the truth is important in any relationship, not just marriage. When people lie and twist things to suit themselves, any relationship becomes strained! If you are the person on the receiving end of lies, you may find yourself constantly doubting the other person. Is he or she telling the truth? And if not, why not? What might the truth be? What is he or she not telling me?

Many people learn from a young age, at home or at school, how to spin events so that they are not blamed. If they can get away with it, lying quickly becomes a habit they take with them into adult life and often into marriage. But distorting the truth, however you try to present it, is akin to lying and needs to be treated as such. The good news is that even adults can learn to tell the truth and accept blame where it is due. We don't have to be perfect all the time. God is merciful, patient and forgiving. But we must admit our mistakes and be determined to change our ways.

Questions for reflection:

* Do you find it hard to tell the truth?
* Was lying a problem in your family?

Prayer:

The truth sets us free and builds trust. If lying is a problem in your life, you can use the following prayer steps to get free.

1. Forgive any parents, relatives or ancestors for whom lying was/is a problem.

2. Ask God to forgive you for continuing in their sin by not taking the truth seriously and lying yourself. Accept God's forgiveness.

3. As a couple, ask each other for forgiveness if you have lied to each other. (This may only apply to one spouse).

4. If your partner has lied to you, bring any pain you feel about it to Jesus. Ask him to heal your hurt.

5. Cut yourself loose from the spirit of lying, and command it to leave you in the name of Jesus Christ. Continue to pray until you feel free.

Negative behaviour patterns

If we are not careful, the negative actions and reactions between us can become repetitive patterns that keep us apart and drain our hope and energy. But they can be recognised and overcome. We have found that most couples have experienced negative patterns in their marriage at some point. You can identify many negative patterns in your marriage by reflecting on your arguments. Are there certain words, looks, gestures or situations that tend to lead to the same old arguments or fights?

Some of these negative patterns can go back a long way. We may have been locked into unhelpful patterns for years. In addition to the negative patterns that have developed over time as a result of our interaction as a couple, we may have brought negative behaviours and attitudes into our marriage. These are an extra layer of disturbance to deal with as we move towards greater unity as a couple.

An example: Growing up with addictions and violence

We have worked with a lot of women who have had what they would describe as a bad relationship with their father. Perhaps he was an alcoholic and prone to violence when drunk. Maya is one such lady. As she grows up, the seeds of a deep mistrust of men are planted in her heart and wrong thinking takes root in her mind. Deep down she fears that all men are like her father, or at least have the potential to end up like him. One day, however, she meets Rob, who seems like a good man. They fall in love and get married. But she has never worked through her relationship with her father. The deep-seated mistrust of men is still there. Although she doesn't realise it, her core belief about men, and by default her husband, is: "Men are irresponsible and can't be trusted or relied upon. It's safer and better for me to do everything myself and not let my husband get too close". She takes the lead in the home and keeps Rob at a safe emotional distance.

In this example, how might Rob react to his wife's verbal or non-verbal message that he is not to be trusted? Well, he will certainly pick up on his wife's feelings. At some level he will get the message that she doesn't really trust him. This is hurtful to any man and usually leads to conflict. While this generic example may seem overly simplistic, it serves to illustrate how negative patterns can be set in motion early in life and what mistrust can do to a marriage.

In order to break this negative pattern, Maya must be willing to look at her relationship with her father and work through how it has affected her. She may need healing from various painful memories. She will also need to forgive her father for hurting and failing her and the family. And she may need to be set free from a spirit of mistrust of men. She may need to ask God and Rob for forgiveness for taking charge, and for controlling her husband with her mistrust. In turn, Rob will need to ask God and Maya for forgiveness if he has responded to her behaviour and signals with anger and aggression, or with passivity and withdrawal.

This is just one example of many possible negative patterns between husbands and wives that we have seen in our work as prayer counsellors over the years. But we have also seen God help countless couples to break their negative patterns and receive their healing and freedom.

The Holy Spirit leads and helps us to discover the obstacles to unity that are buried deep within. He is great at helping us to find and get rid of the 'rubbish' in us that needs to go. He helps us to clean up our lives and our marriage so that we can grow in unity and experience greater joy and contentment together.

Pause for thought

- Is there a negative behaviour pattern in your marriage?
- Do the same situations lead to the same arguments? If so, when did this negative pattern start? Has it been there since the beginning of your marriage or is it triggered by certain words, looks or situations?

Chapter 5

Overcoming obstacles to unity
Introduction to the prayer tools

Having identified obstacles to unity, how do we deal with the sins, hurts and spirits that fuel them? An effective way to do this is to use the healing and freedom prayer tools. We introduce each one in turn in the different sections later on and show you how to use and combine them. We love these tools and have used them to resolve many conflicts in our marriage! In each case, the Holy Spirit showed us where the problem lay, and what steps we needed to take to overcome it and find peace again, as the following personal anecdote shows.

Angry for no apparent reason

One day I, Daniel, felt angry with Esther, but I had no idea why! It seemed that something she said triggered a negative reaction in me that I didn't understand. I said to myself, "I don't want to feel angry all day or blame my wife unfairly. I'll ask the Holy Spirit to show me what's going on inside me!"

As I sat in prayer, I suddenly remembered the school I attended as a child and one teacher in particular. I couldn't immediately see the connection between what I was feeling in the present (anger towards my wife) and the memory. Except that Esther is a trained teacher. But as I thought about it, I realised what the Holy Spirit was trying to tell me! You see, this teacher had often treated our class very unfairly. We were always on edge, wondering who was going to be picked on next and hoping we hadn't done anything to upset the teacher.

It dawned on me that I had never really forgiven that person. And because we had the same teacher every day for three years, a lot of anger had built up deep inside me! I had never talked about it with anyone or let it go. But the Holy Spirit knew that it was still there. He helped me to finally express the injustice of it all. Using the prayer tools, I was able to take my anger to Jesus and lay it at the foot of the cross, and forgave the teacher for terrorising us as a class.

After praying like this, I immediately felt peaceful again. The anger towards Esther was gone, which was a relief for both of us! If I hadn't known that I could ask the Holy Spirit to show me the root of my anger and how to deal with it, I may have stayed in a bad mood all day and ended up fighting.

As this example shows, when we get upset or angry with our partner, it may not be because they have said or done something wrong! It may be that certain words, looks or actions trigger a reaction in us that is related to something else in our lives that we need to work through. Such a reaction could be a sign that we need to forgive someone or acknowledge a past hurt and receive healing.

Many people suppress emotional pain, tucking it away inside rather than expressing and dealing with it properly. But when we do this, instead of healing inside and moving on, we are left with inexplicable anger, resentment and unforgiveness. But the Holy Spirit can show us where our real problem lies. He can heal and set us free!

Generational issues

Sometimes the issues that people struggle with, such as lying, hatred or unforgiveness, have actually been in their family for generations. All sorts of generational 'baggage' like this can weigh us down and prevent us from experiencing the deep love, genuine friendship and close unity we long for.

Prayerful reflection on the family into which you were born can be a helpful step in overcoming generational obstacles to unity in marriage. The Bible says that the sins of previous generations can affect their descendants up to the third and fourth generation (Exodus 20:5). We have seen evidence of this in many couples we have ministered to over the years. Likewise, the tendency to continue in certain sins often passes from one generation to the next – until someone stops it.

It's worth taking a closer look to see if any of the negative traits or behaviour that either of you struggle with in your marriage are present in your family lines. Respectfully consider the lives of your parents, grandparents and great-grandparents and compare them to your own. Did any of them struggle with the same issues as you?

For example, we both had a problem with anger. We could get very angry and hurt each other with our outbursts. It was as if at certain moments something came over us that was not part of us and was very difficult to control. We realised that this strong anger had been present on both sides of the family and we decided to put an end to it. Using the prayer for deliverance in this chapter, we forgave our ancestors for passing the anger on to us as a spiritual inheritance. We repented for continuing in the same sin. We then told the spirit of anger to leave our lives and it went. Since then we have been able to control and deal with anger properly and have not had any major marital conflicts involving anger.

If you are struggling with generational issues that affect your unity as a couple, be encouraged. Like us, you can be set free! We have an enemy in the unseen world who does not want us to be happy together. He wants us to fight, give in to anger and end up disunited, full of hurt and self-pity or even hatred for each other. But God has given us powerful weapons, effective prayer tools that we can use to put an end to his plans and break his power in our lives and marriage.

Sometimes it is easier for a spouse to see negative traits and issues in our lives than it is for us to see them. But if we approach this with mutual love and humility, we may be surprised at what we can identify together. Once we have listed the generational issues at work in our lives, we are ready to bring them to Jesus. Remembering his sacrifice for us on the cross helps us to forgive our parents and ancestors for passing on the same traits to us and for any consequences of their sin that may be affecting us today. It also puts us in the right frame of mind to repent where we ourselves have tolerated and continued in the same sins.

Questions:

- Can you identify any negative traits, sins or issues that run in your family lines?
- Are any of these present in your marriage today? If so, how are they affecting your relationship?

Freedom Prayer

You can use the following prayer tool to bring these issues to God.

1. Tell Jesus what you want to be set free from.
2. Forgive those in your family line who have passed this negative tendency on to you.

3. Ask God to forgive you for repeating the sins of your forefathers.

4. Command the spirit behind this sin to leave you in the name of Jesus Christ.

5. Thank Jesus for setting you free!

Example: Praying about generational anger

To be free from generational anger, the first step is to forgive your forefathers for holding on to anger in their lives. Then ask God to forgive you for continuing the same sin. Ask his forgiveness where you have hurt others with your anger.

You can say:

> *"Dear Lord Jesus, I want to be free from anger! I forgive my forefathers for keeping anger in their lives and for passing this tendency on to me. Please also forgive me for my own anger fits and for hurting others when I was angry. I command the spirit of anger to leave me now, in the name of Jesus Christ."*

When you pray for deliverance, you may feel a physical reaction in your body. This could be a feeling of nausea, or a pressure in your head, stomach or chest that wasn't there before you started praying. You may feel a sudden lightness or sense of relief, or that something is leaving you. We have often experienced deliverance in this tangible way. It is important to keep praying until you feel peace and make sure that the spirit has gone. If it has gone, you should notice a difference. For example, you may find that you can control yourself better in certain situations that would have made you angry before.

Note: You can apply the Freedom Prayer steps to other issues, such as hatred of men or women, fear, need to control, bitterness, and so on.

Six tips for growing in unity
Inspiration for daily life

Practical solutions often go hand in hand with prayers for healing and freedom. We end this section with a list of six things you can do today to help grow the love, friendship and connection between you. We hope this short list will spark your imagination, inspire your own creative ideas and help you to discover what works best for you.

1. Share meals

Sharing a meal creates a sense of togetherness and encourages communication and friendship. Think of meals not just as opportunities to take in nutrients and fluids to keep from collapsing, but as golden moments in your day or week to enjoy being together, to catch up and hear how things are going.

2. Plan a date

Whether you've been married for months or decades, you can still go out on a date together, just like you did before you got married. Some couples forget this! Arrange a time that suits you both and write the date in your diary. And then stick to it. A date doesn't have to be fancy or expensive. The important thing is to make time for just the two of you and do something you both enjoy.

3. Do things together

Many couples do household chores and leisure activities on their own. But this approach can leave little time to spend together as a couple. Instead, try to do as much as possible together and help each other. Plan your free time well. Find out what your partner likes to do and be prepared to accommodate his or her interests so that you do a mix of things that you both enjoy. Planning trips, special activities or holidays together gives you both something to look forward to and helps keep your love fresh.

4. Work on common projects

Focusing on something beyond ourselves can be very enriching. Helping others, contributing to church life, getting involved in neighbourhood projects, supporting charities, or even playing on a local sports team all provide opportunities to grow and contribute. You don't have to do everything together. But take an interest in what your partner is doing and offer support where needed.

5. Look for the treasure

In the process of removing obstacles to unity, it is easy to focus on the negative and what needs to change. Actively remind yourself of the good things in your marriage. Think about your partner's good qualities. What is he or she particularly good at? What do you like most about him or her? Each of us is precious, created by a wonderful God. Even if you have to look a little harder, there will be something beautiful to discover in your partner.

6. Take a walk down memory lane

Think for a moment and ask yourself: Why did I fall in love with my husband or wife? What was it about him or her that I admired or was attracted to? What are my favourite memories of our time together so far?

Take time to celebrate how you found each other and how you still have each other today. Play a favourite song that was meaningful to you when you first got together, or revisit a place that was special to you both. Share memories of when you were dating and of your life as a married couple. Let each other know that no matter what you've been through or what you may be facing: *"You are still the love of my life!"*

Communication

Learning to communicate better

Chapter 7

Laying the right foundations
Communication enables relationship

It was supposed to be the happiest day of our lives. But it felt like the worst. At least for the thirty minutes that I, Daniel stood at the front of the beautifully decorated church, staring into the anxious faces of friends and family who had gathered to witness our union. Or what they hoped would be our union, as my bride had yet to arrive... I clenched my jaw and forced down the feelings of growing anxiety welling up inside me, trying to make myself think rationally. Esther was not known for her punctuality, I knew that. But she had promised me that today, of all days, our wedding day, she would definitely be on time. That left two alternatives. Either she had had a terrible accident on the way to the church. Or she was one of those runaway brides...

Fortunately, neither scenario turned out to be true. Instead, a misunderstanding had led to a delay at the hairdressers. There were no smartphones in those days, so Esther asked someone on their way to the church to let me know she was on her way. But they were distracted by a sudden technical problem and the message was never delivered!

Communication can go wrong for all sorts of reasons, resulting in hurt, disappointment and frustration. Sadly, this wasn't our last communication mishap, and we've had others over the years. Some were exacerbated by the fact that we spoke different languages and came from different cultural backgrounds. But we realised that if we were going to be happy together and have a healing marriage, we had to make an effort to learn to communicate better with each other.

Today we can say that our hard work has paid off. We are at a very different place in our communication than when we took our vows in front of a very relieved congregation all those years ago. We believe that, like us, any couple, no matter how difficult communication may be at the moment, can learn to communicate better with God's help and the right insights and tools.

Good and bad communication

We can communicate on different levels without saying a word. Because communication, is so much more than just talking or listening to each other. We communicate through facial expressions, our eyes, actions, posture, touch, and sexuality. All of these channels of communication allow us to share and connect our lives, and without communication there can be no real relationship.

Good communication skills are not necessarily something we are born with. Many of us have to learn to communicate well. Even before the foundation of the world, God the Father, Son and Holy Spirit have been in communication and relationship with each other. But God also likes to communicate with us human beings, and he does so in many different ways! For example, he speaks to us through creation so that everyone can hear and understand. Sometimes he speaks directly and personally to us through vivid dreams or clear thoughts in our minds. Other times he speaks through circumstances or input from others. But the main way God speaks to us is through his Word, the Bible. So it's no surprise that the Bible has a lot to say about communication! Here are just a few examples on talking and listening:

- *My dear brothers and sisters, take note of this: Everyone should be quick to listen, slow to speak and slow to become angry.* (James 1:19)

- *A gentle answer turns away wrath, but a harsh word stirs up anger.* (Proverbs 15:1)

- *Do not let any unwholesome talk come out of your mouths, but only what is helpful for building others up according to their needs, that it may benefit those who listen.* (Ephesians 4:29)

- *The words of the reckless pierce like swords, but the tongue of the wise brings healing.* (Proverbs 12:18)

- *Let your conversation be always full of grace, seasoned with salt, so that you may know how to answer everyone.* (Colossians 4:6)

- *Sin is not ended by multiplying words, but the prudent hold their tongues.* (Proverbs 10:19)

As these Bible verses show, communication can have a positive or negative impact. What we say and how we say it matters! Both kind and harsh words have power and consequences. Good communication heals and builds up the other person. Choosing the right words and responses can prevent sin and avoid unnecessary conflict. Bad communication, on the other hand, offends and provokes anger. It hurts and drags others down and leads to sin. When this happens between a husband and wife, the result is division and disunity. If unity makes a marriage strong and powerful, disunity weakens it.

By taking steps to heal and improve our communication, we can overcome division and rebuild our unity. And as our unity is restored through better communication, the way is opened for a more beautiful, romantic relationship. Feeling understood by each other is priceless and opens the door to greater sexual fulfilment together. Conversely, romance and sexual intimacy suffer in a relationship characterised by poor communication. If you don't feel understood, you are unlikely to feel very close to each other and the frequency and quality of your lovemaking is likely to suffer.

Pause for thought

- Have you ever had a communication mishap in your marriage?
- Where do you communicate well with each other?
- Where could you improve your communication?

Chapter 8

Prioritising Communication
Good communication is contested

As a couple, we are not immune to the spiritual battle that rages in the unseen realm. We have an enemy who delights in hindering communication and promoting misunderstanding between us, wherever possible. That is his strategy. In the original Greek, the language of the New Testament, this enemy of our souls is called 'diabolos'. This noun comes from the Greek verb 'diabollo' and means 'to accuse', 'to slander', or literally 'to confuse'. When we accuse and blame each other, or speak ill of our partner to others, we do things that weaken or even destroy our marriage. But speaking kindly to each other strengthens our relationship.

We remember preparing to leave Argentina after 10 years. The last few weeks were particularly stressful. We were not sure if our departure was permanent, or if we would return after a few months. Many decisions had to be made and our work handed over fully to local staff. We had to pack up our household and take care of a myriad of other details to leave the country. We also had to prepare for the upcoming visits to the churches in England that had faithfully supported us over the years. With three young children to look after as well, it was a challenging time in our marriage, and our nerves were frayed. There were times when instead of communicating in a friendly way about what needed to be done and who was going to do what, we ended up blaming each other! Later we were able to talk about it and ask for forgiveness where we had hurt each other. But looking back, we know that we could have encouraged each other more if we had communicated better in the first place.

Changing perspectives

Imagine a husband coming home tired and discouraged. He has had a difficult day at work, full of problems and tensions. He doesn't say anything to his wife and tries not to let on that anything is wrong. But inside he is still upset and a little worried about the direction things seem to be taking. His wife doesn't ask him how his day has been and doesn't know he's feeling so bad. From her perspective, everything seems fine!

If we don't tell our partner how we're feeling, or why we're feeling a certain way, there's a potential for misunderstanding, tension or argument. We can easily get upset or angry with them when we are really upset or worried about something else. Instead of explaining that we are a bit nervous for this or that reason, or that we are just not feeling well, we end up hurting them.

If you're a naturally communicative person, you'll probably find it easier to share what's going on in your life and how you feel about it from your perspective. But if you're not naturally talkative, or not used to sharing much with others, you may need some help in this area. Often it is not a question of being interested in others or not, although silence may suggest this. It may just be that you're not used to talking about yourself or your feelings and thoughts, and don't know where to start or what to say.

Similarly, none of us can read our partner's mind, although many of us think we can! So we have to rely on other ways of finding out how our husband or wife is really feeling. One of the best ways is to ask questions. It is a well-known concept that the person who asks the questions leads the conversation. By asking questions, you show that you are interested in the other person. You could start by simply asking your husband or wife what they did that day. Or how their day was. At this point you may just be exchanging information or facts. You can then move to an emotional level by asking questions about feelings. For example, you might ask if something was difficult for them, or how they felt about something someone said to them. Or if they are worried about what has happened, etc.

Avoid bombarding your partner with too many questions, which can quickly feel like an interrogation! Instead, try to find the right moment and learn to ask the kind of questions that convey your genuine interest and concern. Look for opportunities to connect at this level every day, if possible, so that you can keep up to date with how each of you is doing.

Establishing a culture of trust

We once counseled a couple where the husband came from a very poor family where the members rarely spoke to each other beyond exchanging basic information. Although they shared meals together, everyone ate as quickly as possible and left the table to continue working or doing household chores. The lack of communication and connection as a child led to feelings of isolation and loneliness that continued into adulthood. He desperately wanted something different for his own children. He made a conscious decision to create a different culture of communication in his home from the one he had experienced growing up. We encouraged him to start by using mealtimes as an opportunity to talk to his wife and children. By learning to ask simple questions and listening carefully to the answers he received, he was able to create an atmosphere of greater trust and intimacy in his home. He reported that he felt much closer to his wife and children than before.

Perhaps the way your family communicated when you were growing up has influenced the way you communicate with your spouse, children or others today? Like this man, you can choose to make a fresh start. You can take steps now to work towards establishing a different culture in your marriage and home. It is never too late to start. And no step is too small to take!

Pause for thought

- How easy is it for you to find out how your husband or wife is doing and what they are feeling?
- How might influences from your upbringing be affecting communication in your marriage today?
- What kind of communication culture would you like to see in your marriage?

Chapter 9

Overcoming our differences
When two worlds collide

Communication has always been a bit of a challenge for us. Esther grew up in Kenya and England and is a native English speaker. Daniel, on the other hand, grew up in Switzerland and his first language is German. So from the beginning of our relationship we have had to deal with some language and cultural barriers, and we touched on this briefly in the context of unity in the previous section.

Language barriers

We are both naturally communicative and speak each other's languages well. However, we often experienced misunderstandings and were frustrated with the quality of our communication. One day we realised that there was a common thread running through most of our communication problems: We often either failed to communicate important details, or what we did say was not expressed in such a way that the other person could understand it clearly.

Just because we thought we understood the words coming out of the other person's mouth doesn't mean we automatically understood what they were actually saying. Some words can mean different things in different contexts. And even when we are united and feel close to each other, information and ideas are not automatically synchronised between our brains!

The following rule of thumb has helped us to improve communicate and minimise misunderstandings:

- Say what you want to say clearly
- If necessary, say it again in a different way.
- Check with each other that the message and details are clear.

Cultural challenges

Good communication in a cross-cultural marriage like ours, is not just about learning each other's language, although that certainly helps! Paying attention to linguistic and cultural nuances can be just as important in avoiding misunderstandings.

For example, an Englishman might politely indicate that he is cold by saying to his host, "It's a bit chilly today, isn't it?" What he really means is, "I'm cold, would you mind closing the window?" In England, such a comment is likely to be taken for what it is: The visitor doesn't want to impose his will on the other person or cause inconvenience, but he has a need. The host is likely to respond by offering to close the window.

Your average Swiss visitor in the same situation, on the other hand, is likely to simply ask, "Do you mind if I close the window? Or he or she might just get up and close the window without asking. While these are clearly stereotypical examples (there will certainly be Swiss and English people who behave differently), the point is that culture adds a dimension to communication in marriage that we need to be aware of. This can be true even if you come from different geographical regions (of the same country) where people behave differently.

As well as our basic cultural differences, we also have different personalities and communication styles. In previous conversations, Daniel would sometimes say, "Just tell me in one short sentence what you are trying to say!" He wasn't used to people hinting at things and didn't see the immediate relevance of what Esther was trying to say. She felt hurt that he didn't seem to be making an effort to listen deeply or to try to understand her point of view. Then one day it dawned on us that this too was partly a cultural issue! Esther understood that Daniel didn't think it was imposing for her to say certain things directly, and Daniel realised that he needed to look for the meaning behind her words and patiently ask for clarification when necessary.

We heard of a couple who attended a seminar on communication. The speaker outlined the challenges for intercultural couples in a country like Switzerland, with its different languages, dialects and cultures. Suddenly, they understood the source of much of the tension and conflict in their marriage. The wife was from the German part of Switzerland, and the husband from the Italian part. Culturally, they had different priorities in life. She derived meaning from her work, while his relationships gave him value and purpose. Once they realised this, they were able to understand and accommodate each other much better.

Creating your unique marriage culture

When we marry, God creates something new. This includes the opportunity to build a unique culture within our marriage; one based on clear biblical values and principles, while drawing on the best of what each of us brings to the marriage from our backgrounds. When it comes to human traditions and ideas, we may need to be willing to compromise and find a middle ground that we are both happy with. Mutual respect for each other's background and cultural identity is important. We need to learn to be generous and patient, to give each other the space to be ourselves without undue criticism.

At the end of the day, no matter what worlds we come from and how or when they collide, marriage will always require a certain amount of give and take for things to work well. We once met a couple who married late in life, but unfortunately the husband was unwilling or unable to make room in his life for his new wife. He resented any change to his bachelor lifestyle and ended up pushing her away.

Pause for thought

- Are there any language barriers in your relationship?
- Do you face any cultural challenges in your marriage?
- What unique culture would you like to see in your marriage? What steps could you take together to build it?

Chapter 10

Communication killers
What to watch out for

If we are not careful, we can kill a conversation before it has a chance to get going, putting an end to what could have been a fruitful discussion. In this chapter, we look at four common areas to watch out for: Word choice, tone and volume of voice, facial expression and complaining. If we make a conscious effort in each of these areas, not only will our communication as a couple improve, but the atmosphere in the whole family is likely to improve as well.

Word choice

We read in the Bible that death and life are in the power of the tongue (Proverbs 18:21). Our words can bring life or death. That is why the Bible describes the tongue as a fire, a world of evil, with which we praise God and curse others (James 3:3-9).

Certain words and insults can be very damaging to a relationship. We may say things in the heat of the moment that we know will hurt the other person. But we say them anyway. At times like this, our marriage feels like anything but a healing place! The good news is that we are free to choose words that build up our partner rather than words that destroy them. Some people agree with this in theory, but feel they still have the right to say hurtful things in certain situations. This attitude is usually counterproductive and tends to fan the flames of conflict. We have seen many examples in our ministry over the years of this approach spreading like fire through a whole family. Parents and children insult each other back and forth with words they have no right to use. Left unchecked, this can become a deadly habit.

In the early years of our marriage, we too fell into the trap of saying hurtful things or insulting each other in the heat of an argument. But we soon realised how destructive this was to our relationship and decided, with the Lord's help, to stop. We asked for each other's forgiveness and promised not to use certain words, no matter how angry we might be with each other. Making a conscious decision to watch our words has led to greater peace in our marriage. If this is your problem, we encourage you to make a similar decision today.

Avoiding hurtful words doesn't mean avoiding difficult conversations or sweeping disagreements under the carpet. On the contrary, it is important to take the time to talk and iron out our differences. Prepare for such a conversation by agreeing on a time and place that is convenient for both of you. Decide on just one or two topics to discuss together and stick to them. Before you start talking, pray in your heart:

"Holy Spirit, give me your gentle words!" And remind yourself of what the Bible says:

> *Gracious words are a honeycomb, sweet to the soul*
> *and healing to the bones.* (Proverbs 16:24)

Remember that our tone of voice, volume and facial expressions can interact with our words to trigger something negative in the other person. On some level, they may be reminded of a past situation where they faced someone who said something similar or looked or sounded like you. Emotionally, they feel as if they are facing an old teacher, a demanding father, a bossy sister, or whoever it may be, all over again. If you think this might be happening, you may find it helpful to pray together for healing and deliverance from past wounds. We will show you how to do this in the following chapters.

Tone and volume of voice

In many ways, the tone, or the way we talk to each other, is as important to good communication as the words we use. For example, if you say something in an impatient tone of voice, the other person is likely to think that you are annoyed or upset with them. This may or may not be the case. Our job can sometimes have a negative impact on the way we talk to others outside of work. For example, teachers, who are used to giving orders and telling students off, can sometimes come across as bossy outside the classroom. They need to be particularly careful not to use a lecturing tone at home. But even farmers can need help in this area! We once received a call from the wife of a Swiss mountain farmer who was at her wits' end. It seemed that her husband was having trouble distinguishing between his wife and his cows, because he used the same brusque tone with all of them!

Similarly, if your job involves little talking, you may find it hard to switch into a lively communication mode at home, or you may compensate by talking too much! Whatever your situation, it is worth paying attention to how you talk to each other. Be prepared to adjust your tone to avoid hurting or provoking your partner unnecessarily.

Volume also plays an important role in good communication. Talking in a loud voice is often seen as a precursor to aggression and violence. If you know you are going to talk about a difficult topic where things could get out of hand, it can really help to prepare in advance. Think about your tone of voice, how to keep your voice down and how to keep an open expression on your face. You can practise your facial expressions and composure by standing in front of a mirror and imagining possible conversations.

Facial expression

The human face can be very expressive, as you may have noticed! Without saying a single word, our faces can convey happiness, friendliness, interest, empathy, impatience, anger, fear, boredom and much more. In fact, we can communicate much more than we realise through our facial expressions. If we are not careful, we can make another person feel unnecessarily insecure or uncomfortable. They may even get the wrong idea about how we are or what we are feeling.

The Bible has this to say about facial expression:

> *A person's wisdom brightens their face and changes its hard appearance.* (Ecclesiastes 8:1)

If you've never done this before, take a good look at yourself in the mirror. Notice your facial expression. Do you have a bright and friendly face or rather a hard look or appearance? Sometimes we need to allow God to turn our hard features into a smile.

Nagging and complaining

Some people tend to see the negative in everything. As a result, they are always complaining and criticising. They find it hard to see the positive in anything or anyone. Perhaps you know someone like this?! In marriage, such an attitude can be draining and hard to live with. But the Apostle Paul says:

Give thanks in all circumstances; for this is God's will for you in Christ Jesus. (1 Thessalonians 5:18)

We have found that focusing on the negative and complaining all the time can actually make people sick! But gratitude is the best way to overcome a negative attitude, defeat bad moods and break the habit of whining and complaining. As a young man, Daniel had the opportunity to observe the power of gratitude and the devastating effects of negativity in unique circumstances. As a young theology student, he was unable to find suitable accommodation near his faculty in Basel and ended up living in a retirement home! At first he was just relieved to find a room at all, and the tasty food and cleaning service made up for the unusual surroundings. But sharing life and meals with the seniors, turned out to be mutually enriching and enlightening.

During his stay at the home, he noticed two types of residents. Those who were content and had a positive attitude to life. And those who were unhappy, complaining all the time and for whom the staff seemed unable to do anything right. One elderly lady in particular made a lasting impression on him. One day she said, "Danny, life is like rowing a boat. We have to use our right arm to praise God and our left arm to thank Him. When we do both of these things, our boat moves forward!"

What a great picture! And what a profound spiritual truth when it comes to marriage as well. When we praise and thank God for everything, instead of complaining and moaning, He can work in our marriage and help us move forward together.

Pause for thought

Reflect on your communication as a couple:

- What kind of words do you use with each other?
- Do you often end up raising your voice?
- What do you think your face says to your partner?
- Do you tend to nag or complain a lot at home?

Chapter 11

From battlefields to radio silence
Exposing communication abuse

Can you imagine living under the same roof with someone but not saying a word to one another? Years ago, while visiting one of our sponsoring churches in England, we heard of a couple in the parish who had been engaged in a silent war for eighteen years – with no end in sight. They had quarrelled and simply stopped all communication.

The silent treatment

Some people ignore their partner and refuse to talk to them in certain situations, even if they don't keep it up for eighteen years! But deliberately shutting out or stonewalling a partner is hurtful and can have a negative impact on any marriage. There can be many reasons why people behave in this way. It could be out of hurt, an attempt to punish or manipulate their partner to get their own way, or a sense of hopelessness that talking won't make a difference.

Sometimes staying silent can help prevent further escalation or violence. But we are talking about flat-out refusing to communicate with your partner and ignoring them. This rarely solves any of the deeper problems in a marriage.

Tension and conflict may subside for a while and 'normal' conversation resume, but unless we get to the point where we can talk things through and learn to resolve our differences, we are actually storing up trouble for ourselves. Instead of resolving the conflict, the silent treatment hurts our partner and silently adds fuel to the fire. What we are really saying is: "I don't want to talk to you and I'm not interested in resolving our differences. Anyway, I'm not the one to blame, you are. So until you admit your mistakes and apologise, we have nothing to say to each other.

Remember that communication is more than just talking. It can include looks, touch, sex and more. So denying your partner any of these things to punish them, for example, is also a form of communication denial and should be avoided.

Intimidation

Communication can also be used as a weapon of intimidation if we are not careful. Our facial expressions, choice of words and tone and volume of voice can consciously or unconsciously put pressure on our partner to do what we want or to make us feel better at their expense.

As we noted in a previous chapter, our tongues have the power to bring life or death, to make or break our marriage. So what we say and how we say it is important if we are to have a healing and satisfying marriage, where we both feel safe to exchange information, express feelings or opinions and share thoughts and dreams.

Summary

Over the last few chapters we have looked at some of the common barriers to good communication in marriage. Perhaps you have already identified areas you need to work on to improve communication in your relationship? With God's help, you can learn to communicate better. But bear in mind that you may also need some healing and deliverance in the process to deal with hurts from the past that are affecting the way you communicate in your marriage. We are convinced that God wants us to be truly happy in marriage. But it is important that we look honestly at our lives and take the necessary steps to deal with any negative experiences or baggage from our past. This will give us the best chance of building and maintaining a healthy marriage. If we are emotionally healthy, we will have a healing effect on our partner. But if we are emotionally wounded and spiritually bound, we are likely to hurt our spouse and others around us.

Let us recall the warning, and the incredible promise, contained in the verse we read earlier:

> *The words of the reckless pierce like swords, but the tongue of the wise brings healing.* (Proverbs 12:18)

Applied to marriage we could say: If we are healthy on the inside and careful to control our tongues, then our marriage can be a wonderful place of healing, an oasis where our words and the way we communicate bring healing to each other!

Pause for thought

- Have you ever given your spouse the silent treatment?
- Are you guilty of trying to punish, control or manipulate your partner by what you say or how you say it?
- Do you need healing or freedom from past experiences negatively affecting your communication as a couple?

Chapter 12

Communication and conflict resolution
Inspiration moving forward

Improving your communication and conflict resolution skills in marriage can be challenging, but sometimes a few simple steps in the right direction can make a big difference. We round off this section with six tips to help you find the right focus, and to keep moving forward. You won't be able to tackle everything at once, so break things down and set manageable goals. The important thing is to start somewhere, and keep working to improve together.

1. Don't give up!

There are a number of factors involved in improving effective communication. But the first, and probably the most important, is your will. Make a firm decision today that you *want* to learn to communicate better with your spouse! For example, you could decide to:

- Work on understanding any cultural and linguistic differences between you (this isn't always easy and will probably take a lot of patience).

- Keep your voice down and refrain from shouting.

- Avoid giving dirty looks, looking down on your partner or trying to make him or her do what you want.

- Refrain from using bad language or insults, even if you are upset. Your partner is not your punching bag.

- Keep the lines of communication open. Avoid stone-walling or denying sex etc. as a means of punishment.

- Stop complaining, nagging or criticising your partner, yourself or others. Instead, focus on being thankful in all circumstances, as 1 Thessalonians 5:18 teaches.

- Say a sentence or two more. Make sure your partner has the main points and understands what you are saying.

2. Set aside time

Many couples find it helpful to plan a 'marriage' or 'date night' to create space for communication. As you talk and listen to each other, try to relax and look into each other's eyes. Make an effort to share thoughts, feelings and current challenges. What are you both enjoying at the moment? What do you find difficult? What are your fears, hopes and dreams for the future? The idea is to get beyond talking about to-do lists, the weather, or even politics, business, career or religious ideas. While such topics can make for stimulating discussion, sharing feelings, fears and dreams takes communication to a whole new level, and will help you to better understand how your partner ticks.

Watch how you react to the information your partner shares with you. Comments such as, "How could you be so stupid?" or "I'm not surprised you got yourself into such a mess!" won't encourage your husband or wife to show weakness in front of you again! It's hard to open up when you're afraid of being rejected or ridiculed. You can show empathy, even if you don't fully understand their feelings or what they're going through.

This will go a long way to creating an atmosphere of trust and acceptance in your communication.

If we bring the performance mentality of the modern world into our marriage, we are likely to destroy each other, no matter how much time we spend talking. Marriage should be an oasis where we can relax, away from the pressure to be perfect and the stress of everyday life. It should be a refuge where we accept and love each other unconditionally and encourage each other to be the best we can be. When this happens, times of communication in marriage become moments of healing rather than stress.

3. Identify bitter roots

We noted earlier that the will to communicate better is an essential first step to improving at it. A next step is to be willing to identify any bitter roots that may be hindering our communication. Is there a particular topic that you no longer want to talk about with your partner, or one that raises a red flag in your mind whenever it comes up? Could it be that you still have feelings of hurt and have not forgiven your partner for something they have done or said? Or maybe you're just frustrated that talking hasn't made much difference in the past and you just don't feel like trying any more?

The Holy Spirit can show you any bitter roots that may be hindering your communication. He can guide your conversation and help you to reconcile in these areas.

4. Forgive each other

Once you have identified any bitter roots, decide, with God's help, to forgive your partner and let go of the resentment. Pause for a moment to see how you react to this decision. Can you forgive, or is it a struggle? Sometimes it is not possible to forgive immediately. You may need some healing and deliverance before you can fully forgive.

5. Schedule business meetings

Good planning and coordination of tasks can greatly reduce tension and the potential for conflict. Schedule 'marriage business meetings' to deal with the practical details of home and family. Decide what needs to be done, by whom, and by when. Here are some examples of topics you might discuss at such meetings:

- Planning of marriage or date nights
- Planning leisure activities, outings and holidays
- Children or grandchildren's progress, needs and requests
- Needs of aging parents or other relatives
- New purchases
- The cleaning and laundry
- Renovation or repairs to your home
- Gardening and other work around the house
- Car or bike repairs
- Requests from other people to do things
- Meeting with friends
- Church or ministry involvement
- Business related to charities or clubs
- Other...

Before each meeting, make a list of the points you both want to discuss. Arrange a date and time that is convenient to both of you. Agree on the length of the meeting, e.g. thirty minutes or an hour. Stick to your agreed agenda and time frame. Try to come to conclusions and make practical decisions. If you can't reach a decision, agree to come back to the issue at a later date.

6. Be gracious and patient

As we get older, many of us find that we forget things from time to time. We're not that old ourselves, but we've noticed this happening to us and our friends from time to time! Whatever the reason, forgetfulness can sometimes lead to frustration and tension in a marriage.

We may assume that because something is clear to us, it is also clear to our spouse. Then we find out later that it's not clear to them at all. Or that they've simply forgotten some important information that they would normally have remembered. In situations like this, it's very important to be patient and gracious with each other! Going over arrangements quickly before an event or double-checking each other's understanding of a particular issue can help ensure that we are as much on the same page as possible. Writing down important dates and appointments or making a to-do list can also help if memory is an issue.

Pause for thought

- What role can you play in building a culture of trust in your marriage?
- Is there a bitter root that is poisoning your communication?
- How could business meetings benefit your relationship?
- Is forgetfulness a problem in your marriage? If so, how can you help each other to remember things better?

Restoration

Learning to overcome sin

Chapter 13

Nowhere to hide
Facing what's inside

Sophocles, the ancient Greek poet, recounts the tragic story of King Oedipus. Through pride and misjudgement, he ends up killing his father and marrying his mother! In ancient Greek literature, this kind of undesirable behaviour is often described in terms of *hamartia*, which essentially means 'to miss the target'. The ancient world would have been familiar with this term and its meaning. So it's not surprising that the New Testament writers chose this word to describe the concept of 'sin'.

If we're honest, we all make mistakes. We all fail to hit the target of God's best for us and fall short in some area of our lives and marriage. In other words, we are all guilty of sin. And because this is so, we all need forgiveness or cleansing for our sins again and again.

Dealing with the sin is the first of three key areas that contribute to the ongoing restoration of our inner being. The more our inner man or woman is restored, the stronger and more beautiful our marriage will be. We look at the other two areas – healing emotional wounds and deliverance from demonic oppression – in the last two sections.

Falling short

Marriage is probably the one place where our falling short or sinfulness becomes most apparent. Many people can keep up appearances outside the home, at least for a while. But in marriage it is pretty hard to hide things from each other. Sooner or later, our weaknesses and failures will be exposed. In marriage, we are confronted with what's in the depths of our own hearts. But we also get a front-row seat to what's going on below the surface in our partner's life.

Some of what we see may be good and inspire greater love and admiration for each other. But other things may be ugly and harder to deal with. Could it be that the fear of getting too close to another person, of discovering things we would rather keep hidden, is what keeps many people from getting married in the first place, and others from working on their marriage at a deeper level? If we are to flourish in marriage, however, we must be willing to face the truth about ourselves.

We have talked about sin in terms of missing or falling short of the target. But what target are we talking about? The Apostle Paul gives us the answer:

> *For all have sinned and fall short of the glory of God.*
> (Romans 3:23)

The target or goal is holiness, which reflects the glory of God in everything we think, say, do and feel. No one but Christ has ever hit this target repeatedly and can therefore claim to be perfect. The rest of us fall woefully short. A perfect person might be a dream partner, but sadly they don't exist!

The sooner we can accept the true state of affairs, the sooner we can get on with dealing with all the rubbish that is in each of us. If we have not dealt with sinful thoughts, words and actions before we get married, we are likely to bring them with us into the marriage. Sins don't just appear out of nowhere when we get married. Rather, what is already deep within us is forced to the surface by the closeness of our spouse. This is actually a good thing. Because we believe that God's plan for us as married couples is to help each other overcome our sinfulness so that the holiness and glory of God can be restored to our lives and manifested in every area of our being.

The challenge of closeness

In the spiritual realm, a husband and wife have melted together and become a new unity. The Apostle Paul describes this as follows in Ephesians chapter 5 verse 31:

> *For this reason a man will leave his father and mother and be united to his wife, and the two will become one flesh.*

The Greek word Paul uses here to describe this becoming one flesh is *proskollaomai*. This essentially means that as a married couple, we have been glued together by God. As we noted earlier, this closeness or oneness makes it difficult to hide anything from each other. At some point, our negative qualities and weaknesses will come to the surface and become visible. People react differently when this happens. Many people simply accept that the honeymoon period is over and that they will get on each other's nerves and hurt each other; their relationship may even grow cold. Others separate and move on to the next partner. Still others give up on marriage and decide they are better off alone.

A better way to respond is to allow what is not good in us to come to the surface of our lives under the guidance and control of the Holy Spirit. And then to pray for each other. The prayer steps we share later in this section will help us do this. God wants marriage to be a place of restoration and healing. For this to happen, we must be willing to open our lives to his Holy Spirit. Allow him to put his finger on anything that is wrong and needs to be changed.

Restoration is possible

We have found that with determination and God's help, anyone can turn away from sin and be restored. But have you noticed that the world often has little time or patience for people who have messed up? They are quickly judged, found wanting and written off. Perhaps this is because many people don't really believe in change. Beware of this kind of thinking in your marriage; it inevitably leads to division and conflict.

We knew someone who was happily married – or so he thought. One day his wife came home and out of the blue announced that she had had enough of him and wanted a divorce.... This example may sound strange, but some people keep secret records of their partner's misdeeds and hold grudges. Eventually they decide they've had enough and move out, sometimes without any apparent prior conflict. They just get fed up and leave.

Learning to communicate better and to express hurt, frustration or disappointment can certainly help to prevent tragic outcomes like the one described above. But we also need to go a step further and deal with sinful attitudes and behaviour in our marriage. If we make a mistake or hurt our partner in any way, we should be quick to admit it and ask for forgiveness. It is extremely important to forgive and reconcile quickly. If we remain unreconciled for a long time, we run the risk of a bitter root taking hold and spoiling our marriage.

The Bible warns us about this:

> *See to it that no one falls short of the grace of God*
> *and that no bitter root grows up to cause trouble and*
> *defile many.* (Hebrews 12:15)

Pause for thought

- Do you believe that a person can change?
- Are you willing to face what is inside you?
- Do you keep a list (in your head or in your heart) of the wrong things your partner does?

Chapter 14

Recognising sin in marriage
Destructive behavior patterns

The most significant changes in our marriage came when we began to look more closely at the sins in our lives. We realised that what we had thought of as negative character traits, such as anger, impatience, self-centredness or resentment, were actually sins that poisoned relationships. The Bible calls such attitudes and behaviours 'works or acts of the flesh':

> *The acts of the flesh are obvious: sexual immorality, impurity and debauchery; idolatry and witchcraft; hatred, discord, jealousy, fits of rage, selfish ambition, dissensions, factions and envy; drunkenness, orgies, and the like.* (Galatians 5:19-21a)

Again and again we had to make the decision not to tolerate such things in our lives! When the Lord brought a particular sin to our attention, we found it helpful to first study what the Bible had to say about it. We used a concordance to look up all the verses that mentioned that sin to see what God thought about it and how it affected (our) lives. Meditating on these verses prepared us to get to the point where we were really sorry and wanted nothing more to do with that sin! It helped us to truly turn away from it and ask God for forgiveness. Thinking about the consequences of a sin strengthened us to resist the temptation to go back to it. The Bible calls this process 'repentance'. The Greek word for it is *metanoia*, which literally means a change of mind. In other words, a change in our view of sin and our presumed right to continue in our sins. This is the first step towards a marriage marked by love and authentic spirituality.

Main characteristics of sin

How can we recognise sin at work in our life or marriage? Sin has devastating effects. It robs us of peace and joy and destroys relationships. Sin pushes us in the wrong direction, setting us on a path of restlessness that ultimately leads to destruction and spiritual death. But God wants to give us grace and life:

> *For the wages of sin is death, but the gift of God is eternal life in Christ Jesus our Lord.* (Romans 6:23)

Therefore, it is important to be vigilant and alert so that we can recognise sin in our lives and in our marriage and deal with it before it causes too much damage. God, in his great love for us, makes us aware of our sin through his Holy Spirit. He does this not to spoil our fun or make us feel unhappy and judged, but to give us the opportunity to repent so that his life can flow even more through us and in our marriage:

> *...let us throw off everything that hinders and the sin that so easily entangles. And let us run with perseverance the race marked out for us, fixing our eyes on Jesus, the pioneer and perfecter of faith.* (Hebrews 12:1-2)

Start with yourself

Some people have an unusually high opinion of themselves. They consider themselves above reproach and find it difficult to admit mistakes or sin. A person with this mindset will always blame others and rarely look for fault in themselves. This attitude is one of the main reasons why some people have problems with relationships of all kinds and why even Christians end up separating or getting divorced. In our ministry over the years we have met many people whose relationships and marriages have been slowly poisoned by this deadly attitude. In the Sermon on the Mount Jesus says:

> *Do not judge, or you too will be judged. For in the same way you judge others, you will be judged, and with the measure you use, it will be measured to you.*
>
> *Why do you look at the speck of sawdust in your brother's eye and pay no attention to the plank in your own eye? How can you say to your brother, 'Let me take the speck out of your eye,' when all the time there is a plank in your own eye? You hypocrite, first take the plank out of your own eye, and then you will see clearly to remove the speck from your brother's eye.*
> (Matthew 7:1-5)

When it comes to dealing with sin in marriage, Jesus challenges us to start with ourselves. Instead of focusing on our partner's faults, we should first take a long, hard look at ourselves and see where things might not be quite right with us. As we begin to change, our marriage will be positively affected. For example, we may become less irritable. Such a change sends positive signals to our partner. We invite you to make the following verse your regular prayer:

*Search me, God, and know my heart; test me and
know my anxious thoughts. See if there is any offen-
sive way in me, and lead me in the way everlasting.*
(Psalm 139:23-24)

When sin becomes a habit

Sin in marriage often involves both partners because we are
dealing with sinful patterns of behaviour. Sometimes these
have taken root over many years and become strongholds.
This happened to us. We have already mentioned a time when
we were under great pressure before we moved from Argentina to Switzerland. Instead of communicating smoothly, we
ended up hurting each other with our words and actions.
Years later we noticed that we often behaved in the same way
in other stressful situations. It had become a sinful pattern
in our marriage that we needed to deal with. Today we have
learned to discuss the details of what needs to be done and to
trust each other to do our part. We watch our tongues and try
to stay calm in stressful situations.

Sinful behaviour patterns can take many forms in a marriage. For example, one partner may not trust the other in a
particular area of life. They communicate their distrust, consciously or unconsciously, through words, actions or looks.
Their partner senses the mistrust and suspicion and often re-
acts negatively. The same situation triggers the same reaction
over and over again, sometimes for years. In such situations,
it can be very helpful to ask the Holy Spirit to show us any
hidden sinful patterns at work in our relationship and to help
us to overcome them.

Here are some more examples of common sinful behaviour
patterns in marriage that we have observed.

No or poor communication

We mentioned earlier a couple who lived under the same roof but had not spoken to each other in eighteen years. They were caught in a sinful pattern of ignoring and disrespecting each other by refusing to communicate. We also mentioned that some relationships end abruptly with no apparent warning or prior conflict.

To avoid such tragic endings, it is important that we quickly identify and break any sinful communication patterns in our marriage. We also need to learn to communicate well and to make things right when they go wrong, so that we do not become bitter with each other. Other sinful communication patterns include things like name-calling, swearing, shouting, threatening, evil looks, using sex as a weapon, and so on.

False accusations

Couples can blame each other falsely. In other words, they blame the other person for things they are not guilty of. For example, we worked with a couple where the husband kept accusing his wife of not wanting to have sex. As we talked it became clear that he was the main problem: he pushed her to work very long hours and rarely took time to do anything nice or romantic for her. She felt used and pushed him away.

Not owning up to guilt

Some people go to great lengths to hide their guilt and continue to sin. For example, a couple came to us for counselling some years ago. The wife believed that her husband was having an affair with another woman, and she had some pretty compelling evidence to support her suspicions. Instead of admitting that he was cheating, he denied it. Over the next few days, he created chats and social media posts to try and prove his innocence. But he later admitted they were all fake.

Being dogmatic and opinionated

We have come across many couples where one spouse tends to believe that they are always right. This dogmatic attitude is very hurtful and damaging to a marriage. When such a pattern is broken and replaced with an attitude of humility and a willingness to discuss and compromise, both partners can begin to flourish in their different personalities and gifts.

Criticism and fault-finding

When they first start dating, most couples are quick to pay compliments and avoid finding fault with each other. But as life goes on, a critical attitude can creep in. They start to criticise each other more and more, perhaps in front of others. They end up giving their partner mocking or derisive looks, or saying things that make them feel silly or embarrassed. They may make it their business to complain, criticise and scold their partner, sometimes to the point of becoming controlling or even violent. This creates insecurity and tension.

There are many other examples of sinful behaviour in marriage that we could mention. But perhaps you have already identified similar or different ones in your own marriage? If so, you may well be dealing with a sinful pattern that has come to involve both of you, and for which you both now bear some responsibility. Recognising sinful patterns in a relationship, and being willing to take responsibility for your part in perpetuating them, is a first step towards change, and can in itself bring a measure of relief and hope.

Pause for thought

- What sins might you be tolerating in your life?
- Can you see any sinful patterns of behaviour in your marriage?
- Make a decision to stop allowing sin to spoil your life and your marriage!

Chapter 15

Overcoming sin in marriage
Five steps that bring life

We have seen how the sins of one or both partners can lead to sinful behaviour in the marriage. In this chapter we will look at how to deal with and overcome sin once we have identified it. Doing so will go a long way towards breaking sinful patterns between us, and pave the way for learning new ways of relating. Just as God forgives our sins and removes our guilt every time we sincerely ask him, so too can we learn to deal with sin and to forgive one another in marriage, even if it is not always easy. The following five steps will lay the foundation to help you do this.

1. Recognize your sin

The first step in dealing with sin is to recognise that we all sin and that sin spoils our relationship with each other. If you're not convinced that this applies to you, just ask your husband or wife what they think! Often others see our sins and faults more clearly than we do, but that is only human. In the end, however, it is the Holy Spirit who convicts us of our wrongdoings and leads us to the truth about ourselves

(John 16:13). This is medicine for our souls because the truth sets us free (John 8:32).

So why do so many of us find it so difficult to admit our sins and mistakes? There can be many reasons for this. Some people struggle with pride and the fear of losing face. Others have never been taught to do so, like the lady in her early thirties who came to us for help in dealing with her past. Left to her own devices as a child, she had struggled through life as best she could. When she became a Christian, she realised that she had to make things right with certain people. But as she had never apologised to anyone in her life, she had no idea how to go about it.

Another reason why some people find it difficult to admit their sin is that they have adopted a performance and/or perfectionist mindset. Many societies and employers have little time for people who make mistakes. They want perfect production units – or at least it can sometimes feel that way! In Switzerland, as in other countries, there are many well-trained people who don't make many mistakes at work, and everyone is grateful for that! However, this mindset becomes a problem when one spouse imposes the same high standards from work on their family and themselves, creating an atmosphere of tension at home. No one wants to underperform, make mistakes or commit sins, but the fact is that we all do. The sooner we acknowledge where we have fallen short, the sooner we can deal with it and move on.

2. Bring your sin to God

In 1 John 1:9 we read the following liberating truth:

> *If we confess our sins, he is faithful and just and will forgive us our sins and purify us from all unrighteousness.*

Similarly, in the Letter to the Hebrews, the Holy Spirit says:

"Their sins and lawless acts I will remember no more." (Hebrews 10:17)

This is wonderful news for all of us. We don't have to be perfect! We don't have to try to hide or deny our sin any more. We can bring it out into the open and come to God with it. This is what it means to confess our sins. When we do, God promises to forgive us and to remove the stain and the stench of that sin from our lives. Covering things up, or trying to convince ourselves and others that we are innocent when in fact we are guilty, is a waste of everyone's time and energy. How much better to cut to the chase and simply say, "I'm sorry!

3. Ask each other's forgiveness

Having confessed our sin to God and received his forgiveness, we are ready to put things right between us. We have often experienced how liberating this step can be. When we offend or sin against each other, we take time to clarify the situation together and extend forgiveness where necessary. This simple strategy allows us to maintain our peace and unity.

Many people feel uncomfortable talking about sin or guilt. In fact, some couples rarely talk about who is to blame for what, and wouldn't know what to ask forgiveness for. Their relationship may seem harmonious, but they both know that something is not quite right between them. For whatever reason, they choose to sweep things under the carpet.

Other couples have no problem talking about what has gone wrong and who is to blame. But they never get to the point of asking for forgiveness because they end up arguing and going round in circles. Nothing productive comes out of their discussions because they don't have the tools to deal with the problem of sin in their marriage. If this is your situation, you will find the Forgiveness Prayers for couples in the next chapter particularly helpful.

4. Be willing to change

It takes the will and determination of both partners to avoid returning to the same old sins and sinful behaviour patterns. Jesus said in Matthew 18:22 that we should forgive again and again. But he did not mean that we can go on sinning as much as we want to, because our partner has a duty to forgive us anyway. If we are unwilling to change, then we probably haven't repented from the heart and begun to hate our sin. Without real repentance there can be no real forgiveness and no real change.

As part of God's family, husband and wife can also be considered brother and sister. 1 John 2:9-11 warns us therefore not to remain in darkness:

> *Anyone who claims to be in the light but hates a*
> *brother or sister is still in the darkness. Anyone who*
> *loves their brother and sister lives in the light, and*
> *there is nothing in them to make them stumble. But*
> *anyone who hates a brother or sister is in the darkness*
> *and walks around in the darkness. They do not*
> *know where they are going, because the darkness has*
> *blinded them.*

5. Commit to truth

Many marriages are spoiled because people refuse to face up to the truth about who they are and what they have or haven't done. When confronted, they become defensive or try to shift the blame back onto their partner. Others go quiet and begin to withdraw from their partner on an emotional level. If they end up separating, the official version is that they simply grew apart and that no one is to blame.

It is unpopular nowadays, even in some Christian circles, to talk about sin or the need to establish guilt as a prerequisite for forgiveness. We don't want to make people uncomfortable. But sometimes it is necessary to feel uncomfortable in order to be able to repent. In particular, we need to feel the weight of our own sins and all the things we do, say, think or feel that hurt God, our partner and ourselves.

In this process of dealing with sin, we need to be committed to establishing truth between us. We need to learn to get to the bottom of things and find out what really happened. Who is to blame and for what? How else can we ask God's forgiveness, or each other's, in a way that makes sense? But once we have clarity, we can forgive each other, be reconciled and move on.

Pause for thought

- Do you admit sins and mistakes, or do you tend to sweep things under the carpet?
- Can you handle conflict, or do you try to avoid it?
- Is sin and forgiveness something you can talk about as a couple?

Chapter 16

Prayer tool for restoration
The Forgiveness Prayers for couples

We now come to our first prayer tool. It consists of three steps. You can use it to deal with any sin that has come between you and God, or between you and your spouse. The steps are simple but powerful and will enable you to deal with many of the problems in your marriage on your own. We encourage you to use this tool again and again!

Step 1: Confess your sin
You can say:

> *"Dear Lord Jesus Christ, I am sorry for... (be specific about what you did, said or felt that was wrong). Please forgive me!"*

Where necessary, ask your spouse to forgive you.
You can say:

> *"I am sorry that I have wronged and hurt you with my thoughts, words or actions (be specific). I don't want to do so anymore. Please forgive me!"*

The wronged partner can respond:

"I forgive you for what you said or did to me!"

Step 2: Accept forgiveness

You can say:

"Lord Jesus Christ, I accept your forgiveness. Thank you for forgiving me!"

If you feel the need to forgive yourself, you can say:

"I forgive myself!"

When Jesus Christ forgives your sins it is important that you accept his forgiveness. Likewise, when your partner forgives you, you must accept his or her forgiveness. This is the second step whereby we accept the forgiveness we have asked for. Many people still feel guilty even though they have confessed and asked for forgiveness. This changes when they make a conscious decision to accept or receive this wonderful gift.

Some people desperately want to accept God's forgiveness, but they just can't. Perhaps they know they are guilty of great wrongdoing. They loathe and hate themselves for what they have done. Often a special prayer of deliverance is needed where we command the spirit of unforgiveness to leave us. When that spirit is gone, it is much easier to accept God's forgiveness and to forgive ourselves. We will look at deliverance prayers in the final section.

Daniel was asked to visit and pray with a doctor in Argentina who was dying. He had fallen seriously ill shortly after leaving his wife for another woman. His lover had no interest in being with a sick man and quickly left. Much to the doctor's surprise, his wife took him back and cared for him. His wife's forgiveness and sacrificial love for him made his life very hard. He wept bitterly as he told his story to Daniel, but he could not accept God's forgiveness or his wife's. He recognised his sin, but could not forgive himself for what he had done to his wife. He clung to the idea that he deserved to suffer and died in great pain.

Guilt has the potential to torment and destroy us. This is why it is so important to deal with it, not only by confessing our sin, but also by accepting forgiveness.

Note: If you are still struggling to accept forgiveness, you may need some healing for hurts. We look at this in the next section.

Step 3: Put things right

You can say:

> *"Lord Jesus, please show me what I need to put right".*

You can ask Jesus to show you what you need to put right with others, or where you need to make amends. Wait and listen to what the Holy Spirit says. You may also want to discuss this with your spouse. He or she may have some good advice to help you get things back on the right track.

We want to encourage you here to be determined to deal with sin in your life and marriage. Bring your guilt to God and ask for and receive His forgiveness. The Lord is merciful. He will forgive you and help you to change! As sins and transgressions lose their power and hold over you, you will experience restoration in your marriage. This is beautiful and powerful!

Note: You may want to discuss certain issues or situations with a third party. Perhaps you have a personal problem that is affecting your marriage and you both feel overwhelmed trying to resolve it alone. Going to confession and/or counselling with a trusted priest, pastor or counsellor can be very helpful and release restoration and healing. But we must be willing and determined to change. This is the most important requirement for confession or counselling to bear fruit.

> *Therefore confess your sins to each other and pray for each other so that you may be healed. The prayer of a righteous person is powerful and effective.*
> (James 5:16)

Pause for thought

- Can you accept forgiveness?
- Can you forgive your partner?
- Is there anything you need to put right between you? Practice using the Forgiveness Prayers to do this.

Chapter 17

Hitting the target
Learning to resist and stay connected

Some people repent and make an effort to make amends. But they soon find themselves drawn back to the same old sins! So how can we learn to resist sin effectively and avoid falling back into old sinful patterns?

We believe that the key to resisting the sin that so easily lurks at our door is to cultivate Christian fellowship as a couple. What do we mean by this? On the one hand, we have fellowship with God as individuals when we draw near to him in our personal times of prayer, Bible reading and worship. But we also need to spend time with God as a couple. You may have heard the popular saying, "A couple that prays together stays together!" For years, we've cultivated the habit of spending time with God every day, both individually and together. In Psalm 119:11 we read:

> *I have hidden your word in my heart that I might*
> *not sin against you.*

We read God's Word daily so that we can hide it in our hearts and allow it to transform us and to keep us from the destructive snare of sin. The Bible contains much wisdom and practical instruction on how to live as a couple and how to relate to others. As we read it, we can also ask the Holy Spirit to correct us and show us any hidden sins we may not be aware of and help us to overcome them.

We don't have to try to deal with sin on our own. The Bible says that the Holy Spirit dwells in us. He is the one who strengthens us and gives us the victory over sin – even sin in marriage. In Galatians 5:16 we read:

> *So I say, walk by the Spirit, and you will not gratify*
> *the desires of the flesh.*

In other words, it is our fellowship or communion with the Holy Spirit, combined with the knowledge and application of God's Word, that enables us to effectively resist sin individually and as a couple. Aligning ourselves with the Gospel of Jesus Christ brings peace and tranquillity to our lives and our marriage:

> *Blessed are those whose transgressions are forgiven,*
> *whose sins are covered.* (Romans 4:7)

King David in the Bible was someone who succeeded spectacularly in some areas and failed miserably in others. But when he became complacent and neglected his relationship with God, he ended up sliding into adultery with the woman next door. When Bathsheba became pregnant, David tried to cover his guilt by having her husband Uriah killed (see 2 Samuel 11). When confronted with his sin and the consequences of what he had done, he was completely shocked. He came to his senses and finally cried out to God for forgiveness. You can read his prayer of repentance in Psalm 51.

We have also made it a habit to pray David's prayer regularly for ourselves and as a couple. We want to give God the opportunity to show us where we need to change before we end up in a mess.

Before you read on, we invite you to make the following verses your personal prayer as well:

Hide your face from my sins and blot out all my iniquity. Create in me a pure heart, O God, and renew a steadfast spirit within me. Do not cast me from your presence or take your Holy Spirit from me. Restore to me the joy of your salvation and grant me a willing spirit, to sustain me. (Psalm 51:9-12)

Pause for thought

- How do you cultivate fellowship with the Lord on a personal level?
- How do you cultivate fellowship with God as a couple?

Healing

Learning to heal inner wounds

Chapter 18

The power of healing in marriage
Called to heal one another

Over the years we have become increasingly convinced that God wants to enable us as husbands and wives to identify and heal the inner wounds that are spoiling our marriage. As we do this, our marriage is transformed into a wonderful place of healing and friendship!

When we first got married, we both had some experience of healing prayers. But we had no idea how important such prayers would be to the success and happiness of our own relationship and journey together. Knowing how to effectively heal our wounds has been one of the most significant factors in enabling us to grow together in love and unity. We are excited to share our knowledge and tools with you in this section. We believe your marriage will be similarly renewed and strengthened as you begin to understand and step out to pray for healing for one another.

God's provision for healing

You may have personal or shared wounds from the past or present that are negatively affecting your marital relationship. These wounds may be superficial or deep-seated. You may have many wounds or just a few. You may know exactly who hurt you, when and how. Or maybe things are a little unclear, but you feel that you're not as emotionally healthy as you'd like to be, and that there are some 'tender spots' inside.

Whatever the situation, God sees our pain and our need for healing. No inner wound is hidden from his sight, and no wound is too ugly for him to heal. In Psalm 103:2-3 we read that it is the Lord himself who heals all our infirmities:

> *Praise the Lord, my soul, and forget not all his*
> *benefits – who forgives all your sins and heals all your*
> *diseases.*

God has provided a way to deal with our sins and transgressions, as we saw in the last section. But he has also opened the way for us to become emotionally and physically whole as well! We read in Isaiah 53:4a and 5b that the Lord personally carried our pain on the cross and his wounds bring us healing:

> *Surely he took up our pain and bore our suffering,...*
> *and by his wounds we are healed.*

In this section we discover together how to apply what Jesus did for us. We learn how to pray for ourselves and for each other so that the healing Jesus died on the cross to bring can happen in our lives and in our marriage. We focus on three healing prayers that are at the heart of our approach. You can use them to heal emotional hurts and painful memories, and to deal with your negative reactions to these hurts.

Healing is for everyone

Many people think that emotional healing is only for those with deep or complex wounds. So if they've had a fairly happy life and never experienced anything like trauma or abuse, for example, they don't immediately think that they might need emotional healing. Similarly, others may be aware of inner pain in their lives, but tend to either accept it or play it down. After all, others have suffered far more than they have, and they don't want to complain or draw attention to themselves.

The truth is that many situations can hurt us and leave us wounded on many levels. If left untreated, even a seemingly trivial, superficial wound has the potential to fester and negatively affect our lives and those around us. That's why it's important to take hurts of all kinds seriously and learn to deal with them as soon as possible, as the following generic example shows.

Imagine a boy who is often made fun of at school. The mean words and taunts that his classmates hurl at him every day cut deep and hurt him inside. If no one notices his suffering, offers comfort and helps to stop the bullying, he will be left to deal with the situation on his own. Chances are that he will start to reject himself. He may begin to believe lies about his basic worth as a person, such as: "There must be something wrong with me for people to treat me this way. No one wants to be my friend, so I must be worthless and boring. I'm an embarrassment, so I'd better be careful not to draw attention to myself".

Now imagine that this boy grows up, glad to leave the schoolroom behind him. He falls in love and marries the woman of his dreams. But the inner wounds have never been treated. The lies he believed about himself at that time are still firmly embedded somewhere in his mind. Gradually, the poison from his past begins to seep out and affect his present, especially his relationship with his wife. For example, his deep sense of insecurity is reflected in an inability to deal with his wife's suggestions or criticisms without getting upset. Or in an infuriating need to try to please everyone, even if he comes up short and ends up feeling resentful.

This is obviously a simplified example to show how emotional wounds from the past can negatively affect our marriage today and need to be healed if we are to grow and move on. If we are honest, at some point in our lives we have all been hurt by different situations and people. But God wants to heal us and do something new. As we read on, let us open ourselves to the Holy Spirit and allow him to show us anything in our lives that still needs healing.

Emotional wounds

Inner wounds can be small and superficial, or complex and deeper. We may be able to shake off some hurts easily enough, while deeper wounds may require emotional healing. Many things in life can hurt us and we all react in different ways. We may have wounds from situations and people in the present, in the near or distant past, or even going back to the time of our conception.

We have prayed with many people who have experienced rejection at a young age. Others were rejected by their parents at birth or in the womb because they were not the boy or girl they had hoped for. Being rejected for being the 'wrong' sex is one of the most painful wounds we have encountered in our ministry. But we have also prayed with abortion survivors who were born with wounds from what they experienced in the womb.

Then there are many possible painful experiences in childhood or adolescence, such as the loss of a parent through divorce or death. This can leave a great sense of insecurity. Again, many children experience rejection within the family. A parent or guardian has made them feel less intelligent, less beautiful, less athletic, simply not as good as their siblings.

Others were neglected, spoilt, mistreated, bullied, abused, ridiculed or never taken seriously as children. Perhaps a parent suffered from mental illness or addiction. They grow up feeling afraid and ashamed. They may find it hard to believe that they can do anything right and bring this inner belief into marriage. Finally, many people carry pain from previous relationships or marriages and fear that their current relationship will not last either.

Why time doesn't heal all

Just as a physical wound or cut needs to be disinfected and allowed to heal to prevent bacterial infection, so emotional wounds need to be cleansed to prevent spiritual infection. A spiritual infection occurs when negative reactions to the hurts, such as unforgiveness, bitterness or hatred, mix with the emotional pain and the wound begins to fester. Just as infection in untreated physical wounds has the potential to spread throughout the body and cause great damage or even death, so a spiritual infection has the potential to spoil or even destroy a marriage. This is why it is so important to learn how to heal present and past wounds. And to have our healing tools ready so that we can quickly deal with future hurts.

People who have not learned to deal with hurt tend to suppress or rationalise it. Others prefer to ignore the hurt, hoping that time will heal their pain. Unfortunately, neither of these strategies is ideal or effective in the long run. In our experience, situations of pressure tend to bring the pain of an unhealed wound to the surface, triggering other negative reactions. For example, unhealed pain often manifests as anger, hatred and unforgiveness and can poison any relationship. Unhealed or spiritually infected wounds can also lead to or fuel negative behaviour patterns. We look at this in more detail in the next chapter.

Pause for thought

- Have you brought any pain or hurt from your past into your marriage?

- Do you feel hurt about anything in your marriage today that might need healing?

- What do you usually do when your spouse or someone else hurts you?

Chapter 19

Breaking negative patterns of hurt
Change is possible

Two weeks before our wedding, we attended a marriage preparation course in Switzerland. Most of the other couples there had six months or even a year to go before their big day, so we must have looked a bit disorganised! But the truth was that we were living in two different countries right up until our wedding. There were no online courses or videoconferencing in those days, so we decided that a last-minute course was better than no course at all.

We have never regretted our decision to attend the course because it opened our eyes to the danger of negative patterns taking root in a marriage and wreaking havoc. The course leaders encouraged us to make a decision that if we ever hurt each other, we would always talk to each other as soon as possible and pray together about what had happened. We made that decision and it has proved to be right to this day.

The truth sets us free

If we are not careful, as we have seen with sin, hurt and our reactions to hurt can also lead to negative patterns in our marriage. These strain our relationship, but Jesus said:

Then you will know the truth, and the truth will set you free. (John 8:32)

Realising the truth about our feelings and behaviour opens the way to freedom and healing. This is good news!

Obviously our lives didn't start when we got married. We had a life before we got married! In that life we may have been hurt and hurt others. We can bring those hurts into our marriage, as we saw earlier. As a result, certain words or actions that our spouse says or does can trigger something in us. We are consciously or unconsciously reminded of another painful situation in the past. This can make it very difficult for us to deal rationally with the present situation. We become upset or angry, perhaps even losing control or lashing out at our partner, even though he or she may have no bad intentions towards us. Reactions like these can add fuel to the fire, increasing tension and inflicting new wounds, so that we find ourselves in a vicious circle. If we don't push back, negative patterns of hurt can become entrenched.

We have seen many examples of this in couples we have counseled over the years. The following generic examples are intended to help you better understand the negative impact behaviour patterns of hurt can have on the marital relationship. While the biographical details will differ from person to person, the resulting behaviour patterns are often similar.

Common examples of negative behaviour patterns:

* A man grows up spoiled and dominated by his mother. He enters marriage with a passive attitude and is easily intimidated. As a result of his passivity, his wife takes charge, a role she increasingly resents. This leads to frustration and hurt on both sides.

* A woman grows up with an alcoholic father who cheats on her mother. The lies, aggression and infidelity she

witnesses leave her with a deep sense of disappointment and insecurity. Because of what she experienced with her father, she enters marriage with a suspicious and negative view of men. She unconsciously projects her father's destructive behaviour onto her husband. She expects bad things from him, leading to frustration, hurt and recrimination on both sides.

As we can see, when two people get married, they may bring with them a rucksack full of pain, anger, rejection, self-rejection, hatred and many other negative emotions that are related to their previous lives and relationships. In this way the experiences of the past negatively affect their marital relationship in the present.

Pushing back on negative patterns

Destructive patterns resulting from hurts and reactions to hurts are a sign that we are not quite whole in some area of our marriage. The sooner we recognise this, the sooner we can begin to push back against these patterns and move towards change. We can start by looking at our own responses. Do they suggest that we or our partner may be carrying an inner wound in some area? The aim is to identify any negative patterns that are affecting our marriage and then to overcome them in prayer:

> *Therefore confess your sins to each other and pray for each other so that you may be healed. The prayer of a righteous person is powerful and effective.*
> (James 5:16)

It is easy to react badly to what our partner says or does, even though we know they are operating from a place of hurt. Unfortunately, this tends to lead to conflict and we end up hurting each other even more. When things escalate, we may not even know what triggered the conflict in the first place!

Such patterns or chain reactions are sadly common. Repeatedly experiencing them can cause people to lose heart, avoid marriage or give it up. Instead of being the place of healing that God intended it to be, marriage is seen as a prison where you are beaten and cornered. If we don't have the tools to deal with hurt and conflict, it's hard to sustain a deeper relationship. Often the best thing to do seems to be to withdraw or escape. But later we find ourselves just as lonely and isolated. We don't want to commit to another person or invest in relationships that are bound to be short-lived anyway.

This is where God wants to meet and heal us today! He wants to give us new hope and the assurance that we can make a success of our marriage. The more whole we become, the more each of us can contribute positively to our relationship – and the more time we will want to spend together. Feeling obliged to spend time together when you would rather not, knowing that you will only end up hurting or criticising each other, or making excuses to avoid being together, will become a thing of the past!

It's never too late: James and Linda's story

This is the story of a couple we ministered to some time ago. They have allowed us to share their experience as an example of how emotional wounds and the patterns they create can threaten the success of a marriage, but that it is never too late to pray for healing – even if the wounds are decades old:

"We have had enough! If God doesn't heal us, we will have no choice but to separate...". After almost forty years of marriage, Linda and James (names changed) were exhausted, disappointed and desperate. They had made many attempts to work on themselves and their relationship over the years, but little had changed in the key areas. James was passive, content to leave things to his wife and had difficulty expressing his feelings. Linda was hot-tempered and had taken charge from the start. The problem was that the older she got, the less energy and strength she had to do what she used to do, and the more resentful she became of her husband for not pulling his weight. If they were honest, neither Linda nor James really wanted to separate. They longed to be more united and clung to the hope that God could help them find peace and a way to make things work.

We explained to them that negative patterns in marriage often have their roots in emotional hurts and spiritual bondage. God knows exactly what those roots are and we can ask him to show us. We invited them to work with us using this approach, and they readily agreed. Each time they came for counselling, deep, hidden wounds from their childhood or marriage came to the surface.

One of the most important roots the Lord revealed was an incident that happened in the early weeks of their marriage. In a frightening incident outside their home, Linda was the victim of an attempted sexual assault. She confided in James about what had happened, seeking his comfort and protection. But because of certain experiences in his own childhood that came to light as we talked and prayed together, James was completely overwhelmed and paralysed by the situation. As a result, he was unable to show empathy or take further steps to protect her. His reaction shocked and hurt Linda deeply. She responded with anger, bitterness and suspicion. After all, it wasn't the first time in her life that a man had attacked her and those she trusted had looked the other way. Her husband seemed to be no different....

At the time, neither Linda nor James had the tools to deal with such a situation, so they tried to put the terrible ordeal behind them as best they could and move on. But Linda was never able to fully open her heart to her husband again. Something was deeply broken between them.

Using a combination of the prayer tools in this book, this deep wound and other related wounds to it were finally healed. Their relationship has changed dramatically as a result. James reports that he has become more proactive and is happy to take the initiative. Linda is learning to trust her husband and to let go. Their relationship is one of love and respect. They have even begun using the prayer tools on their own to pray for each other where needed. They have finally found the peace and unity they longed for: "We are still the same couple, but our relationship has been made totally new by the power of Christ at work through the healing prayers!"

Pause for thought

- Is there a negative pattern of hurt in your marriage? Ask the Holy Spirit to show you what is fuelling it.

- Together: Ask for forgiveness where you have hurt each other through your words or actions. Ask God to forgive and heal the hurt.

Chapter 20

Healing past and present wounds
The Hurts Prayers for couples

We have seen how we can get emotional wounds, and why they need healing if we want to enjoy deeper unity, love and friendship in marriage. Perhaps you have already been able to identify some hurts in your life or relationship? The question now is, how can you deal with those hurts, so that they no longer bother you, and you can grow in love and friendship together? We believe that, as spouses, we can minister healing and freedom to one another. Learning to use the Hurts Prayers we offer in this chapter is an important key to help you do this effectively.

A healing marriage in progress

When the Holy Spirit shows us wounds in our lives, or in our partner's life, and we know how to pray for healing, then God can use us to heal even the deepest of wounds. Read James 5:16 once again:

> *Therefore confess your sins to each other and pray for each other so that you may be healed. The prayer of a righteous person is powerful and effective.*

What an incredible verse! We have already seen how we can ask for and receive forgiveness for our sin in the previous section. This corresponds to the first part of the verse: *"confess your sins to each other"*. Having done that, we are ready for the second part of the verse: *"...and pray for each other so that you may be healed."* Our task then is clear: *"pray for each other so that you may be healed."*

We don't need to follow any particular words or rituals when we pray for healing. But many people find it helpful to work with a prayer template. This helps them to understand and internalise the principles of healing and apply them to their situation. That is why we have written the Hurts Prayers and the other prayers in this book. We want to give you adaptable tools that you can use again and again. Our hope and prayer is that as you begin to use these tools, you will experience the healing power of God transforming your marriage into a place of great healing, just as we have!

Using the Hurts Prayers

What can we do when we feel hurt or irritated, for example? A good place to start is at the root. This may be related to a past or present pain.

Ask yourself:

- Why do I feel hurt? Is it because of something my partner said or did to me that was wrong?

- Or is it something deeper, related to something else entirely, the emotional memory of which was triggered by what my partner said or did?

If it is simply that your partner has hurt you by saying or doing something wrong, then try to talk about it. If your partner recognises where he or she has gone wrong, he or she has the opportunity to apologise and forgiveness and reconciliation can take place. For example, a spouse asking for forgiveness in this situation might say "I'm sorry I was impatient or snapped at you because I was tired." To which you can respond, "I forgive you!

Ephesians 4:26-27 says the following:

> *"In your anger do not sin": Do not let the sun go down while you are still angry, and do not give the devil a foothold.*

Many conflicts can be resolved with this simple approach. Things get complicated, however, when one partner is genuinely sorry for what he or she has said or done, but the other partner simply cannot forgive. This can be a sign that there is something deeper going on that we need to look at more closely. Often there is a bitter root connected to a past wound. If this is the case, we can go a step further and ask the Holy Spirit to show us exactly where the bitterness and unforgiveness is coming from.

Prayer to the Holy Spirit:
You can say:

> *"Please, Holy Spirit, show me (or show us) why I feel so hurt and resentful and can't forgive".*

Then, take a moment to wait and listen to what the Holy Spirit is showing or saying. Perhaps a memory or a particular thought will suddenly come to mind. Often the Holy Spirit will show us that the hurt or resentment etc. that is preventing us from forgiving our partner has nothing to do with them, or even with our marriage, but with a painful situation in the past. In this case, use the following healing prayers to ask the Lord to heal your pain. We have seen that many inner wounds can be truly healed when we go through these three simple prayer steps. You can use them together or on your own.

THE HURTS PRAYERS FOR COUPLES

Step 1: Tell Jesus what hurt you.
You can say:

"Dear Lord Jesus, I feel hurt because...."

It is important that we express our true feelings about what has hurt us. When we come to Jesus we can be completely honest. There is no need to try to play things down or be strong in his presence. In fact, if we allow our pain to come up, God has the opportunity to heal it! This is the next step.

Step 2: Ask Jesus to heal your pain.
Our Lord Jesus had many hurtful things said and done to him when he was on earth. He knows what it is like to be rejected, ridiculed, mocked, falsely accused, abandoned and even tortured and killed.

You can say:

*"Dear Lord Jesus Christ, you were hurt by other
people. You bore my pain on the cross. This gives
you the power to heal my pain. I give it to you now.
Please heal me!"*

As you pray this prayer, you may suddenly begin to feel an actual physical pain in your heart or body. This is the emotional pain coming up. You can put your hand where it hurts and say:

"Thank you Jesus that you are healing my pain!"

Note: Be careful not to move on from this step too quickly. Give the Lord enough time to heal the pain completely!

We love this part of the Hurts Prayers. We have experienced ourselves and seen with others that Jesus really does bring real comfort and lasting healing here. Often he appears to the wounded partner in a picture they see in their mind or spirit. Or they may suddenly experience his unmistakable presence and peace. However Jesus heals, it is always wonderful to witness the Lord healing our spouse! Many couples experience this for the first time when they come to us for counselling, and it gives them courage and hope to continue to pray for each other in this way at home.

Once the hurt has been healed and the partner being prayed for has peace, you are ready to take the next step, which is to forgive the person who hurt you.

Step 3: Forgive the person who hurt you.
You can say:

"I forgive... for what he or she said or did to me!"

Forgiveness is not always easy. Many people struggle to forgive. But forgiveness frees us from the treacherous desire for revenge and restores our peace. Unforgiveness, on the other hand, spoils our relationship with God. In fact, when we do not forgive, we set ourselves up to be tormented by negative feelings and thoughts and by very real demonic powers. In the parable of the unmerciful servant, Jesus describes this state as a prison. He shows that forgiveness is the only way out (see Matthew 18:21-35).

If your pain has been healed, but you can't forgive, you may need to pray for deliverance. In this case, you can command the spirit of unforgiveness to leave you until you can forgive.

We will look at praying in this way in more detail in the next section on deliverance.

At the end of these three steps, if you no longer feel the pain and have been able to forgive, you can say:

"Thank you, Jesus, for healing my pain!"

Note: If you still feel pain and forgiveness is difficult, you can repeat the three healing steps, or move on. Sometimes it is necessary to pray for the healing of memories, or to deal with our reactions to hurt, or to pray for deliverance first in order to receive complete healing.

Pause for thought

- What inner wound do you want to bring to Jesus?
- Do you notice when your partner feels hurt or is not doing so well?
- Are you ready to try the Hurts Prayers together?

Chapter 21

Dealing with negative reactions
The Reactions Prayers for couples

We have seen how we can bring emotional pain to Jesus as a couple. But this is only the first part of effective healing. The next stage is to deal with our reactions to what our partner has said or done to us. These reactions they can cause further hurt and fuel the conflict. Imagine that one of you has had a bad day or is just not feeling well and says something unguarded and hurtful. The other person can't let it go and says something hurtful back, and you end up arguing. If this sounds familiar, you're not alone!

Many of our reactions to hurt are understandable and human. We may even be able to justify them. But holding on to them actually causes more problems. Dealing with our reactions, on the other hand, is like applying disinfectant to a wound. It kills the unwanted germs, and allows the wound to heal properly.

Taking responsibility for our reactions

Many people never get over what has been done to them. They hold on to reactions of bitterness, anger, pain and unforgiveness, sometimes for years. As with physical wounds, a kind of infection sets in and prevents complete healing. This condition can be called a 'spiritual infection'.

If we are to move forward, we need to address our reactions to hurt. Many of the negative responses to hurt, such as hatred, unforgiveness, self-pity, etc., lead to sinful behaviour. Ephesians 4:31 warns us:

> *Get rid of all bitterness, rage and anger, brawling*
> *and slander, along with every form of malice.*

Rather than holding on to such reactions, and allowing them to ruin our lives, it is much better to deal with them! The following prayer tool will help you to break the power of negative reactions to hurts, and rid yourself and your relationship of their poison.

THE REACTIONS PRAYERS FOR COUPLES

Step 1: Tell Jesus how you feel about what happened and how you reacted.

If you have said or done something wrong because you felt hurt, confess it to the Lord.

You can say:

> *"Dear Lord Jesus, I feel…because of what my partner*
> *said or did to me. It was unkind and unfair. But I*
> *also said or did unkind or unfair things back because*
> *I felt hurt."*

It is important to express our reactions to hurts honestly. Talking to God about our reactions to what has hurt us is not about wallowing in negative feelings, or dwelling on the hurt, or even trying to justify our reactions. This would encourage a victim mentality, which we certainly don't want! Rather, telling God openly and honestly how we feel helps us get to a place where we can actually allow Him to help us deal with and break the power of our wrong reactions. Some reactions to hurt can be so strong that we are in danger of hurting ourselves or our partner if God does not help us deal with them.

Step 2: Ask Jesus to forgive you for your reactions and for holding on to them.

Tell Jesus that you are sorry for thinking, saying, or doing wrong things as a result of your reactions to the hurt.

You can say:

> *"Lord Jesus, please forgive me for the way I reacted and for holding on to these negative feelings and reactions."*

When we are hurt in marriage, we often react badly ourselves. We then become a perpetrator and not just a victim. It can be liberating to recognise and admit that this has happened. Acknowledging that we have reacted badly to hurt in marriage or other situations in no way diminishes or excuses what has been done to us. Nor does it give anyone a licence to continue to hurt us! But it does protect our hearts from the bitter roots and false victimhood that are so common today. It also allows God to heal us so that we can truly put past and present pain behind us and move forward together.

Step 3: Ask Jesus to take away the negative feelings.

You can say:

> *"I ask you Lord Jesus to take away these negative feelings (name them). I let go of them and give them to you!"*

You may find it helpful to imagine yourself standing next to Jesus. See yourself giving Him all your negative feelings and reactions to the hurt.

When they are gone, thank Jesus for your partner and bless him or her:

You can say:

> *"Thank you, Jesus, for (name)! I bless him/her in your name!"*

Pause for thought

- How have your reactions to hurt caused you to hurt yourself or others?

- Where have you become bitter or said hurtful things?

- Deal with any wrong reactions using the Reactions Prayers.

Chapter 22

When memories torment us
The Memories Prayers for couples

We now come to our third prayer tool, the Memories Prayers for couples. Structured in a similar way to the healing and reactions prayers, this tool offers another way of accessing our inner wounds and allowing God to heal them.

As we become aware of hurts we have brought into the marriage or situations where we have hurt each other, it can be helpful to invite God into the painful memories associated with these hurts. God is not bound by time and space, so it is no problem for him to come in and heal painful events in the past. The Memories Prayers position us to receive his healing for both simple and deep wounds.

Some hurts or painful memories may be very tangible, while others may be repressed or even forgotten. But until they are healed, they can continue to negatively influence our thoughts and actions. The beauty of the Memories Prayers is that any pain or negative reactions we may have experienced at the time the memory was created can come to the surface of our lives and be healed by the power of God. And when a painful memory is healed, we find that we can still remember what happened, but it no longer hurts!

We find this prayer tool invaluable. We have used it together to pray through many painful events in our past. Each time we have been amazed at how the Lord has healed and set us free. We have marvelled at the kind of things the Holy Spirit has brought to light that were hidden – and at the change that the release and healing of these things has brought to our lives. The following story is just one example.

Surprised by the Holy Spirit

For many years, as an adult, Daniel felt strangely anxious when it got dark outside, but he didn't know why. One day the Holy Spirit surprised us by taking Daniel back in his memory to the reptile house at Zurich Zoo. It was always quite dark in that building, and as a young boy, he was afraid of the big crocodile. He remained in prayer, he began to experience the same feeling of anxiety and fear that usually came over him when it got dark. But suddenly he saw a light. We told the spirit of fear to leave him until Daniel felt free. The next day, as it began to get dark, he noticed that the strange feeling was gone.

THE MEMORIES PRAYERS

Step 1: Ask Jesus to take you back to a painful memory
You can say:

"Dear Lord Jesus, please take me back to the painful memory you want to heal!"

Then wait and see what God brings to your mind. It's amazing what sometimes comes up when we pray in this way. The important thing to remember is that Jesus is a gentleman. He will never bring up something that is too painful for you at the moment. In our experience, the right memories always come up at the right time, and they are the ones that need healing at that moment!

Once the memory is there, allow the feelings associated with it to surface. Inviting Jesus to take us back to a painful memory usually means experiencing the same feelings of pain, fear, anger, hatred, loneliness, etc. that we felt at the time the painful event occurred, even though we are now in the present.

It is important to allow enough time for feelings to come up during this step, and not to try to pull ourselves together. Otherwise the negative emotions may sink back down without being properly healed and continue to bother us.

Step 2: Ask Jesus to come into the painful memory
You can say:

"Please Lord Jesus, come into this painful memory."

This step is not about imagining Jesus doing something or trying to convince ourselves that we can see him doing this or that to heal us. Rather, we invite Jesus into a situation and give him the opportunity to actually come in and reveal himself to us in that moment. This is very different from simply thinking positively about the past or imagining different endings to certain situations.

Jesus really does have the power to come into our painful memories and work miraculous healing! We have seen this time and time again in our own marriage and with countless people we have ministered to. It is the very presence of the risen Saviour and the revelation of himself to us in a painful moment that brings a healing and freedom that could never be achieved by positive thinking or well-meaning advice.

Jesus reveals himself and heals in many different ways. In the example we shared earlier, Daniel saw a light, which we believe was the light of Christ. Many people who pray this prayer actually see Jesus doing something that comforts, protects or otherwise touches them deeply. Others simply experience the deep, tangible peace of God that cannot be explained in words.

> *Peace I leave with you; my peace I give you. I do not give to you as the world gives. Do not let your hearts be troubled and do not be afraid.* (John 14:27)

Step 3: Express forgiveness

If you have been hurt by someone in the memory that has come up, you can say:

> *"I forgive... for what he or she said or did to me. And I ask you, Lord Jesus, to forgive me for...(name your reactions to the hurt)."*

When you feel peace, think about the painful memory again. Ask yourself, "How do I feel now?"

If you are not quite there yet, remain in prayer in the presence of God a little longer until you feel his comfort and peace. Then thank him for healing this memory.

Note: To be completely free from a painful memory, you may also need deliverance prayers. We come to these in the following section.

Pause for thought

* Do you have a painful memory that you would like Jesus to heal?
* Use the Memories Prayers to bring this memory to Jesus and invite him to heal you.

Deliverance

Learning to pray for freedom

Chapter 23

The power of deliverance in marriage
A key to tangible change

When we talk about deliverance, we are referring to a spiritual process that takes place in the unseen or spiritual realm. However, it leads to very real and tangible change in the seen world of our thoughts, feelings and actions.

If we want to experience the life-changing power of deliverance, we must first understand the reality of the unseen world around us and its influence on our marriage. This will help us to recognise our need for deliverance prayers and prepare us to take hold of the victory over darkness that God has already won for us in Christ Jesus.

A glimpse behind the scenes

If you have a Western mindset, the idea of a being surrounded and influenced by an unseen world might be new to you. This was the case with a man we will call Jack, who Daniel coached here in Switzerland a few years ago. Jack was an alcoholic and his addiction had caused many problems in his marriage. He did not believe in God, but appreciated the contact he had with Daniel. One day, Jack was walking down a deserted street when he passed a bar. He had no intention of going in, but suddenly he heard a clear and audible voice which said, "Come on, let's go in and have a drink together!" He looked around to see who had called out to him, but there was no-one there. The street was still empty. Jack was so shaken by this experience, that he immediately went to see Daniel to ask him what he thought about it.

Now Jack was mentally healthy and had a good job. Since he didn't believe in God, he didn't believe in an invisible or spiritual world either. But when an audible voice, which he knew could not have been human, spoke to him out of nowhere, his eyes were suddenly opened and he was horrified. He realised that a foreign power outside himself had been trying to manipulate him, like a puppet on a string, into hitting the bottle. Before this experience, Jack had prided himself on being independent-minded and self-determined. Suddenly he realised that, when it came to drinking, he was not in control, but that something was controlling him.

As Jack discovered, whether we believe in it or not, whether we like it or not, there is an unseen realm, a spiritual dimension around us that is very real. This tangible world is not all there is! But the good news is that, if we belong to, love and follow the Lord Jesus Christ, we are by no means defenceless against the spiritual forces that are part of this unseen realm.

God has given us the victory
The Bible teaches us that God has already defeated the devil and all the powers of darkness under him once and for all through the death and resurrection of his Son, the Lord Jesus Christ. Moreover, he has equipped us with the necessary spiritual tools we need to protect ourselves, and our marriage, from any attacks coming against us from the unseen world.

Problems in the natural, visible world can have a spiritual component, as our friend struggling with the pull of alcohol in the anecdote above discovered. The realisation that this can be so should not frighten us, but rather give us hope and courage. Because we suddenly realise that things we have accepted as part of life, or perhaps just the way we are could actually change. And that if we could overcome and get rid of the spiritual influences from the unseen realm bothering us, then we would be free!

How deliverance changed our marriage

As with healing, we had some experience in deliverance ministry when we first got married. We had both received deliverance for ourselves and it had made a tremendous difference to us. But we had also prayed for others to be set free and had seen many lives changed.

As we mentioned earlier, the intimacy of married life brings to the surface that which needs to be restored in each of us. So we too soon found ourselves confronted with inner issues and unhelpful behaviour patterns. It became clear to us that there were spiritual components to what we were facing. If we wanted our marriage to flourish, we needed to pray for each other to be set free. Praying for deliverance quickly became as important to us as praying for healing and forgiveness!

Esther recalls one of our first experiences of praying for deliverance together, which happened shortly after we were married: "Daniel was about to give me a hug when suddenly my arms flew up in front of my head, as if to protect me from someone. Now, we knew that I had never experienced violence or physical abuse, so this reaction seemed very strange. We decided to ask the Holy Spirit to show us exactly what was going on. In prayer, I remembered an incident from my early childhood in Kenya. A man who worked in the house next door tried to abuse me. Fortunately, my mother was looking for me and called out to me. When the man heard her voice, he quickly let me go.

Using the Memories Prayers we shared previously, I was able to receive healing from the Lord for this experience. We then went on to pray for deliverance, commanding any spirit that had gained access to my life to go. I actually felt something that was not part of me leave me. Since praying for healing and deliverance for this incident, I have never again had such a reaction when Daniel tried to hug me. We were also amazed to find that the tension I had previously experienced around our sexual intimacy was also gone and I was able to open up to Daniel much more".

The changes we experienced in our marriage as a result of these early prayers paved the way for us to pray together for healing and deliverance in many other situations. From the comfort of our own home, we have been able to effectively help each other overcome many issues in all sorts of different areas as they have come to the surface in our lives.

We are still excited when we think of the change that is possible when we pray for deliverance. And combined with healing and forgiveness, deliverance can overcome many more issues in a marriage than we ever thought possible!

Pause for thought

- Do you believe that the unseen or spiritual world can influence your marriage?
- Is there an area of your marriage where you suspect powers of darkness are at work?

Chapter 24

The spiritual realm around us
God gives us the victory

When we face problems in our marriage and seek solutions, it is important to understand that, not only are we surrounded by an unseen world, but that there is a spiritual battle going on in that realm. As human beings made in the image of God, we are at the centre of it.

The apostle Paul talks about this battle in his letter to the Ephesians:

> *For our struggle is not against flesh and blood, but against the rulers, against the authorities, against the powers of this dark world and against the spiritual forces of evil in the heavenly realms.* (Ephesians 6:12)

In other words, as well as the angels that many people like to talk about, there are also evil spirits. The Bible describes them as fallen angels. They were once good but have fallen away from God. Instead of serving God, they are now fighting against Him. They attack us in an attempt to bring us down and cause us to turn away from God as they did.

The highest-ranking fallen angel is known as Lucifer or Satan, and many believe that he was once an archangel. There are therefore not one, but two spiritual kingdoms in the unseen world. The first is the kingdom of God, with myriads of angels. It is a kingdom of light and of the Son of God, Jesus Christ. The second, is the kingdom of darkness, where the fallen angels gather around Satan. They have risen up against God in the hope of one day defeating him. However, through the cross of Jesus Christ, Satan and all his demons have been defeated and disarmed. In Colossians 2:15 we read:

> *And having disarmed the powers and authorities,*
> *he made a public spectacle of them, triumphing over*
> *them by the cross.*

Understanding that the enemy is disarmed is vital when it comes to praying for deliverance from his attacks. The knowledge that Jesus Christ overcame and defeated Satan through his sacrifice and blood on the cross is fundamental; without it, there can be no deliverance. What Jesus accomplished for us through his death and resurrection is the foundation of our salvation and the basis for our healing and deliverance.

The philosopher Friedrich Nietzsche once made a tragic statement about the Christians he had met: *"In order that I might learn to believe in their Saviour they ought to sing better songs, and his disciples ought to look saved-like."* [1] Believing in salvation and experiencing salvation are not the same, and don't produce the same results. If salvation remains head knowledge, but we never experience the power of God, then our faith can quickly become a tense affair. We believe that God not only wants to give us the faith to believe in him for our salvation, but he also wants to equip us with the necessary

---

1 Friedrich Nietzsche, "Thus spake Zarathustra", translated by Alexander Tille, (New York, The Macmillan company, 1896), 125

tools to work out and experience that salvation on every level, including our marriage!

Jesus first gave these tools to the twelve disciples when he sent them out with the power and authority to expel all demons and to heal diseases (see Luke 9:1-2). God then made them available to all believers through the outpouring of the Holy Spirit at Pentecost. And they are still available to us today! We can use them in our marriage to heal and set each other free so that even Nietzsche, if he were alive today, would see the results and conclude that our Saviour indeed lives and has saved us! So let us learn to assess situations in our marriage from a spiritual perspective, and to select the right prayer tools along with any practical solutions that make sense.

A ministry example

To illustrate what using these tools can look like and the difference they can make, let us tell you about friends we will call Rosa and Miguel, in Argentina. When we first met them, they were not married, but they had young children the same age as ours. One evening over dinner, as we talked about life and love, Miguel shared his ambivalence about tying the knot. On the one hand, he really wanted to get married. On the other hand, he was afraid because his parents' marriage had been so difficult. He didn't want to risk a marriage certificate destroying the love and friendship between them.

We explained to Miguel that the pain he felt about his parents' relationship could be healed. And that he could be set free from the fear that marriage would destroy their love. We offered to pray with him and he gratefully accepted. That very night, the Lord healed his pain and delivered him from the fear that was holding him back. Soon after, he proposed to Rosa, and they were married!

Deliverance as part of every day life

Jesus Christ came to give us life in abundance (John 10:10). In other words, he is for us and when he designed marriage he wanted it to be beautiful and bring us great joy! But Satan, our enemy, wants to steal from us, to kill and destroy whatever he can in our lives, and so he attacks us at every opportunity (1 Peter 5:8). This is a sad spiritual reality, even if we don't always want to hear it. And that's why it's important to add deliverance tools to our marriage toolkit so that we can successfully fend off the enemy's attacks and experience life and marriage to the full.

Just as we brush our teeth every day to keep them clean and avoid dental repairs, we can use deliverance prayers in our daily lives to help us stay spiritually clean and healthy. It may seem a little strange to compare deliverance with brushing your teeth. But there are bacteria on our teeth that we can't see. They have the potential to cause very real pain and damage to our teeth if we don't get rid of them by brushing carefully. To help children understand the importance of brushing their teeth, bacteria are sometimes portrayed as 'tooth devils'. In the same way, we can't see evil spirits or demons, but they are there, constantly looking for ways to attack and spoil our lives and marriages. We need to regularly protect our souls and bodies from spiritual attacks, and swiftly get rid of any invaders that slip through our defences. This is a key to great emotional, spiritual and physical health.

Deliverance under fire

Satan tries many different strategies to make life difficult for us as a couple, and to prevent us from discovering the tools of deliverance that could help us. Common strategies the enemy uses to keep people bound include:

- Ignorance and unbelief
- Fear of the devil
- The idea that deliverance prayers are complicated
- The belief that specialists are needed for deliverance

It is important that we learn to see these strategies for what they are, and learn to successfully defend ourselves against the attacks of the enemy. The deliverance prayers we present in this book are an effective and powerful tool for doing this.

As you begin to step out and pray for deliverance in different situations, you are creating opportunities for God to show his power. The victory he has already won for you on the cross becomes a reality in this area of your life and marriage. You will experience more and more that Jesus really is stronger and greater than the evil one. And that he has the power to set you free from fear, pain, trauma, addiction, sickness and much, much more. The freer you and your partner become, the less tension you will experience in your relationship and the greater the peace and unity between you will be. Your faith will be strengthened and you will be better able to recognise and defeat future attacks from the enemy as well. This has been our experience, and we are convinced that God wants to give you the same discernment and victory in your marriage.

Pause for thought

- Thank Jesus that he came to give you abundant life!
- What is the enemy's strategy to keep you from praying for deliverance? Are there others?

Chapter 25

Identifying and closing entry points
Preparing for freedom

A lack of inner freedom can generate tension in a marriage, which all too often leads to conflict. This is why it is important that we learn to listen to the Holy Spirit, discern the root of problems and pray for healing and deliverance where necessary.

It is a beautiful thing to minister to your spouse and see them healed and set free from baggage that has weighed them down from their childhood, youth or past relationships. We believe that God's heart for marriage is that we learn to pray for and with each other so that we can be of even greater use in the Kingdom! What a wonderful relief it is when things from our past that have kept us from growing together in unity and love come to light. We have talked a lot about this, but it is good to keep the goal in mind.

An important step towards achieving the goal of wholeness and freedom is to understand how evil spirits can gain access to our lives. We won't attempt to list all the possible ways here; that would be beyond the scope of this book! Rather, we want to alert you to some of the main areas of potential spiritual attack in the unseen world. We build on the material covered in previous sections to show you the role of deliverance in dealing with sin and receiving lasting healing so that by the end of the book you should understand each of the five prayer tools and be ready to start using them with confidence.

Spiritual attacks

Spiritual attacks are like darts or arrows that the Enemy throws at us to try to discourage us and rob us of our victory in Christ in every possible area of our lives. One way we know we might be under spiritual attack is when we just don't feel like ourselves, or we don't act, think or feel as we normally would. For example, have you ever had an argument that escalated, but afterwards neither of you had any idea what you were arguing about? It was as if the conflict had suddenly arisen between you, but was not really a part of you. We have certainly experienced this many times. We learned to take a deep breath, calm down and ask God to show us what was behind the argument. Sometimes it was stress, or because we had not had enough time for intimacy. But often it was because God wanted to use us to minister to others and the enemy tried his best to disrupt our friendship and unity first.

We can recognise some spiritual attacks immediately, while others are harder to discern because they are much more subtle. We have trained ourselves not to look at situations only through our human eyes. We want to give God the opportunity to show us how to pray in each situation so that he can also give us the victory in Christ. Sometimes he gives us practical solutions. Other times he will point out our need for forgiveness or a change of attitude. He may also show us that we are under attack in the unseen world and that we need to take authority over any spirit coming against us and command it to leave. When we pray for deliverance in this way, we may yawn, burp, or just start to feel lighter inside. We then feel better and like ourselves again.

Lastly, curses are another type of spiritual attack worth mentioning here. Sometimes curses are sent by other people who are deliberately trying to harm us.

Sin opens the door

A significant entry point for spiritual attack in marriage is sin. If we don't repent and turn from it, we make ourselves spiritually vulnerable and the enemy can gain access to our lives and our relationship. Unforgiveness, anger, resentment and hatred are examples of sins that are often linked to unhealed hurts.

Another important entry point is when other people sin against us, for example by being manipulative or domineering, and we don't feel free from them. But spirits can also come through the family line. They can be behind a tendency towards certain sinful behaviours, such as irascibility, adultery, addiction, etc. Inherited traumas are also common. We have prayed with people whose parents suffered from war trauma, for example.

An essential part of preparing for deliverance is therefore to be willing to rid ourselves of any known sins, and to want to forgive others who have sinned against us or our ancestors.

Emotional wounds

Another common entry point for demons is through untreated emotional wounds. In previous chapters we have seen how important it is to heal emotional wounds in order to avoid spiritual infection. But we won't always have managed to do this, so we need to understand a little more about what spiritual infection is, and the role of deliverance prayers in cleaning out such wounds so that they can finally be healed.

Spiritual infection occurs when the pain of an emotional injury is not healed and negative reactions such as anger, unforgiveness or bitterness are added to it. Evil spirits can take advantage of such a situation to come in and reinforce or intensify our negative feelings, thoughts or actions. For example, if someone has natural anger, they can learn to control themselves and keep their anger in check. But someone with a spiritual infection will find it very difficult to control their anger using natural strategies. Instead of controlling their anger, it begins to control them. Similarly, the person who begins to hate someone who has wronged them, and finds that their hatred just keeps growing to the point where they can't let go or forgive, may need to be set free from a spirit of hatred.

Identify where we are not free

How do we know if there is an evil spirit in our lives, or if we are just dealing with natural emotions or even a bad character? Often we don't necessarily realise that we are under the influence of such a spirit. So the key to recognising where we are not free is to remember that an evil spirit is a separate entity, an independent being. It is not a fundamental part of us, our character or our personality. So again, one of the signs is that we don't feel quite ourselves in some area of our lives. Time and again in counselling people have described certain moments when they felt influenced or controlled by something that just didn't feel like themselves. Others have said that it was as if something came over them. Even though they fought it with all the natural means at their disposal, they could not get rid of it. If a spirit entered us very early in life, it may have become intertwined with our personality or character, but we begin to realise that this is not necessarily how God created us.

If one spouse is not free in one area, it affects the marriage relationship. Although we become one flesh by entering into the marriage covenant, we are still two individuals with our own free wills. So when it comes to properly identifying entry points and then praying for deliverance, the will of the partner who needs to be set free must be involved. In other words, we have to want to be free.

Pause for thought

- In what areas of your life do you not feel totally free?
- How does your lack of freedom affect your marriage?

Chapter 26

Praying for deliverance in marriage
The Deliverance Prayers for couples

We have seen many people experience real and lasting change when they began to use the deliverance prayers, either alone or as a couple. Most have just had the courage to step out and start, even though they may not have felt very confident at first and were cautious about praying for deliverance.

It is right to have a healthy respect for the Enemy in terms of understanding that we can do nothing against his power without the help and protection of our Lord Jesus Christ. Having said that, those of us who are in Christ and live according to his commands have nothing to fear, for our life is hidden in Christ (see Colossians 3:3). Moreover, he has given us the mandate and authority to resist the evil one (see Luke 9:1-2). And not only to resist, but also to drive out any evil spirits that have gained access to our lives (see James 4:7; Mark 16:17). We have the right, power and authority to pray for deliverance and set captives free. We don't do this alone. God is with us by the power of His Holy Spirit. He leads and guides us as we pray and delights in setting us free!

Let us now look at the Deliverance Prayers themselves. As with the other prayer tools, we have three simple and powerful steps. You can use this tool to pray for yourself and each other, whenever you don't feel spiritually free.

THE DELIVERANCE PRAYERS

Step 1: Tell Jesus what you want to be set free from

You can say:

"Dear Lord Jesus, I want to be free from ..."

Name what you want to be set free from. For example, "I want to be free from fear, control or compulsion." Whatever we are struggling with, we can talk freely to the Lord about it. His ears are always open for us.

Our will is crucial here. We must be determined to be free and make up our minds that we will no longer tolerate this spirit and any associated sin in our lives. We must be desperate to be free! If we pray half-heartedly, we will not be set free. Why do we stress this so much? The answer is because God respects our will. And our will has the power to determine our present and our future.

Step 2: Clarify and deal with guilt

If a spirit has come into your life through what someone has done to you, forgive him or her.

You can say:

"I forgive... for what he or she did to me"

If it is your fault, ask Jesus to forgive you for opening the door to this spirit in your life.

You can say:

"Lord Jesus, please forgive me for what I did, said or thought..."

Deliverance is about removing any legal rights the enemy may have to be in our lives. Receiving forgiveness for our sins and forgiving others who have hurt us are important keys to this. In fact, we have never seen anyone set free without repentance and/or forgiveness. The same goes for hurts and wrong reactions that have led to spiritual infection. This is why it is important to look at an issue or problem holistically, using a combination of prayer tools where appropriate. We look at this in more detail in the next chapter.

Step 3: Command the evil spirit to leave you in the name of Jesus Christ

You can say:

"I command the spirit of... (e.g. fear, anger etc.) to leave me in the name of Jesus Christ!"

We noted earlier that an evil spirit is a spiritual being without a body. Therefore, when we command a spirit to leave us, we will often feel it manifest itself in our body briefly before it leaves. For example, we may feel a pain or pressure in our head, a pressure on our chest, heavy feet, and so on. We may also feel the negative emotions associated with the spirit, such as fear, anger, etc., that it has been increasing in our lives. Don't worry if this happens to you. Keep going and keep your will engaged as you command the spirit to leave you.

Continue to pray in this way until the manifestation or the negative emotion you felt has gone and you feel free. You may also experience a sudden peace, joy or lightness in your spirit when the evil spirit has gone. There are a number of ways you can test to see whether the spirit has gone or whether you need to pray more. For example, if you have prayed to be delivered from a spirit of unforgiveness, think about the person you have been unable to forgive. Can you forgive them now? Or if you prayed to be set free from a spirit of intimidation working through another person, think about that person. Do you still feel intimidated by them? When a spirit has gone, you should feel a change. In other cases you may not experience an immediate change. But, over the next days, you will begin to notice that you react differently in certain situations than you did before you prayed for deliverance; perhaps you are able to control your temper better, or sleep peacefully without nightmares.

Finally, always take a moment to thank God for setting you free!

You can say:

> *"Thank you Lord Jesus for setting me free! Fill me afresh with your precious Holy Spirit!"*

Summary:
These three prayer steps provide a simple and powerful deliverance tool that you can use to deal with the spiritual dimensions of issues that are negatively affecting your life and marriage in the unseen realm. We encourage you to use the deliverance prayers at home. You can do this either alone or together whenever you recognise that you need to be set free in a particular area of your life. Remember that you can combine the deliverance prayers with the other prayer tools for a holistic approach to your journey to lasting healing and freedom.

Chapter 27

Getting better results
Combining prayer tools

Craftsmen often have a variety of valuable tools at their disposal to work with. Their knowledge and experience allows them to select the right tool for the job. When they are finished, they sit back and inspect their handiwork. Filled with joy and a healthy pride, they are grateful for the gift they have been given – for the strength and skill to create something new, or to restore something that was old or broken. Their hard work has paid off! They have built something of great beauty to enjoy now and to inspire future generations.

In the same way, you can use the five healing and deliverance prayer tools we have discovered together, alone or as a couple, to create something new, refresh the old or to repair that which is damaged. The five tools are:

1. The Hurts Prayers
2. The Reactions Prayers
3. The Memories Prayers
4. The Forgiveness Prayers
5. The Deliverance Prayers

We have found that combining the tools in different situations gives us the best chance of dealing systematically and effectively with issues that threaten our unity and love. So how do we know where to start or which prayer tools to choose?

The best way to do this is to look closely at the situation or problem that is bothering you. Ask the Holy Spirit to help you understand what is going on and to show you where to start. Resolving problems often requires a combination of practical solutions and change, as we talked about in the sections on unity and communication. The Lord can help you identify areas to work on and give you creative solutions. He will also open your eyes to the spiritual dimensions of issues and what needs forgiveness, healing and deliverance. You will often need to use not just one, but a combination of prayer tools to get the best results. The following list will help you make the right choice.

Checklist for choosing prayer tools

Situation	Tool	May also need
You have been hurt	Hurts Prayers	Reactions Prayers Deliverance Prayers
You have reacted wrongly to hurt	Reactions Prayers	Deliverance Prayers
You have a painful memory	Memories Prayers	Deliverance Prayers
You have sinned	Forgiveness Prayers	Deliverance Prayers Hurts Prayer
You do not feel spiritually free	Deliverance Prayers	Hurts Prayers or Memories Prayers

The more you understand the principles behind the healing and deliverance prayers, and the more you get used to using the tools, the more natural it will feel to use them. As you become increasingly whole, your love, friendship and unity as a couple will grow. This has been our experience, and the experience of many we have helped! And by the way, you can also adapt these prayers and use them with children and teenagers to heal the whole family. We explain more about how to do this in our book, "Parents Empowered".

Finally, look to the Holy Spirit in every situation. He will show you roots of issues, and how to combine and apply the prayers in your situation. We encourage you to use this approach again and again. It's worth it, and we know you'll be thrilled with what the Lord does and the results you get!

Appendix

Prayer Tools for Married Couples

THE FORGIVENESS PRAYERS

Steps:

1. Confess the sin
2. Accept forgiveness
3. Put things right

You can say:

1. *"Dear Lord Jesus Christ, I am sorry for... Please forgive me!"*

   To partner: "I am sorry that I have wronged and hurt you with my thoughts, words or actions (be specific). I don't want to do so anymore. Please forgive me!"

   Partner responds: "I forgive you for what you said or did to me!"

2. *"Lord Jesus Christ, I accept your forgiveness. Thank you for forgiving me!"*

   Where necessary: "I forgive myself!"

3. *"Lord Jesus, please show me what I need to put right."*

THE HURTS PRAYERS

Steps:

1. Tell Jesus what hurt you

2. Ask Jesus to heal your pain

3. Forgive the person who hurt you.

You can say:

1. *"Dear Lord Jesus, I feel hurt because..."*

2. *"Dear Lord Jesus Christ, you were hurt by other people. You bore my pain on the cross. This gives you the power to heal my pain. I give my pain to you now. Please heal me!"*

3. *"I forgive... for what he or she said or did to me!"*

THE REACTIONS PRAYERS

Steps:

1. Tell Jesus how you feel about what happened and how you reacted.

2. Ask Jesus to forgive you for your reactions and for holding on to them.

3. Ask Jesus to take away the negative feelings

You can say:

1. *"Dear Lord Jesus, I feel... because of what my partner said or did to me. But I also said or did unkind or unfair things back because I felt hurt."*

2. *"Lord Jesus, please forgive me for the way I reacted and for holding on to these negative feelings and reactions."*

3. *"I ask you Lord Jesus to take away these negative feelings of .... I let go of them and give them to you.!"*

THE MEMORIES PRAYERS

Steps:

1. Ask Jesus to take you back to a painful memory
2. Ask Jesus to come into the painful memory
3. Express and receive forgiveness

You can say:

1. *"Dear Lord Jesus, please take me back to the painful memory you want to heal!"*
2. *"Please Lord Jesus, come into this painful memory."*
3. *"I forgive... for what he or she said or did to me. And I ask you Lord Jesus to forgive me for....(name your reactions to the hurt)."*

THE DELIVERANCE PRAYERS

Steps:

1. Tell Jesus what you want to be set free from
2. Clarify and deal with guilt
3. Command the evil spirit to leave you in the name of Jesus Christ

You can say:

1. *"Dear Lord Jesus, I want to be free from ..."*
2. *If someone has sinned against you: "I forgive... for what he or she did to me."*

If you have sinned: "Please Jesus, forgive me for what I did, said or thought…"

3. *"I command the spirit of…(e.g. fear etc.) to leave me in the name of Jesus Christ!"*

Help for you and your marriage

The spiritual tools presented in this book work for both young and older couples. You can adapt them to suit your situation. Use the prayers as provided, or choose your own words. You can come to Jesus alone or as a couple and allow HIM to heal you and lead you both into greater freedom!

About the authors

Daniel was born in Zurich in 1966. He holds a Masters in Theology from the State-independent Theological University of Basel (STH). Further postgraduate studies at Trinity College Bristol included marriage counselling. He was ordained an Anglican Deacon in 2002.

Esther was born in Kenya in 1973 and moved to England at the age of seven. She studied Hispanic and African Studies at the University of Birmingham and has a Post Graduate Certificate in Teaching from the University of Bristol.

Daniel and Esther were married in 1995, having known each other for most of their lives, thanks to the long-standing friendship between their mothers.

From 1998 to 2007 they worked as mission partners in Northern Argentina, helping families and couples to grow in love and friendship with God and each other, especially through healing and deliverance ministry.

In 2013 they founded Bethesda Heilungsdienst, a ministry dedicated to helping people become emotionally, spiritually and physically whole in Christ.

Contact and online information

Do you need more support?

We believe that any couple who applies the prayers and principles presented in this book can experience real change. Some people find it helpful to talk and pray with someone else. You can find out more about our counselling services and resources on our website.

Did you enjoy this book?

Write and tell us how the book has helped you. We would love to hear from you!

You can play an important role in helping other couples find healing and freedom by recommending this book to your friends and sharing it on social media.

Many people rely on book reviews to help them decide whether or not to buy a book. Please consider leaving a short review on the platform where you purchased your copy.

If you ordered from Bethesda Heilungsdienst, you can email your review to us at the address below. Thank you very much!

bethesda-heilungsdienst.ch
info@bethesda-heilungsdienst.ch

Another book from the authors

"Parents Empowered: Healing and deliverance with kids and teens"

In this book you will discover how to build a heart-to heart relationship with your child and create a healing atmosphere in your home. Drawing on examples from their own parenting and over twenty years extensive prayer ministry, including with families, Daniel and Esther show you how to discern problems and help children and teens deal with issues before they take root. Learning to overcome issues enables children to develop their own practical faith and to flourish now and into adulthood.

Print: ISBN 9783952512708
Ebook: ISBN 9783952512715

Available from bethesda-heilungsdienst.ch or wherever books are sold

More on healing and deliverance

"Ministering Below the Surface: The ultimate guide to simple and effective inner healing and deliverance ministry"

This book will help you understand the principles of Christian healing and deliverance ministry and empower you to help yourself and others. Born out of decades of anointed ministry, this book deals with the roots of problems rather than just the symptoms. It involves a combination of insights, decisions, prayer steps and the supernatural work of the Holy Spirit. It is suitable for the individual or group study.

Authors: Albert & Elisabeth Taylor, David M. Taylor

Print: ISBN 978-1724095534
Also available as an Ebook

Available from bethesda-heilungsdienst.ch or wherever books are sold